BREAKING THROUGH

Making Therapy Succeed
for YOU

For

Deborah Aguado

Nancy Chandler

and

Terry Kirgo

BREAKING THROUGH

Making Therapy Succeed
for YOU

by Dee Gregory

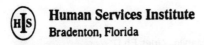

Human Services Institute
Bradenton, Florida

TAB BOOKS
Blue Ridge Summit, PA

Copyright © 1990 by Dee Gregory

FIRST EDITION
FIRST PRINTING

All rights reserved. No part of this book shall be reproduced, stored in a
retrieval system, or transmitted by any means, electronic, mechanical, photo-
copying, recording, or otherwise, without written permission from the publisher. While every precaution has been taken in the preparation of this book,
the publisher and author assume no responsibility for errors or omissions. Neither is any liability assumed for damages resulting from the use of the information contained herein.

Library of Congress Cataloging-in-Publication Data

Gregory, Dee.
    Breaking through : making therapy succeed for you / by Dee
Gregory.
      p. cm.
    ISBN 0-8306-3549-1
    1. Psychotherapy—Popular works. I. Title.
RC480.515.G74 1990
616.89'14—dc20   90-31457
                                       CIP

TAB BOOKS offers software for sale. For information and
a catalog, please contact TAB Software Department, Blue Ridge
Summit, PA 17294-0850.

Questions regarding the content of this book
should be addressed to:

    Human Services Institute, Inc.
    P.O. Box 14610
    Bradenton, FL 34280

Development Editor: Dr. Lee Marvin Joiner, Ph.D.
Copy Editors: Pat Holliday and Pat Hammond

Cover photograph by Susan Riley, Harrisonburg, Virginia

Contents

Contents

Foreword

We could *all* use "Breaking Through." It will be of particular help to those people who feel, emotionally, like "the hole in the doughnut" and who don't know precisely what the problem is, or where to begin looking for help.

In all my years' experience of facilitating groups and assisting people in their search for appropriate help, it has become clear to me that the combination of therapy, self-help groups, and individual writing exercises is often useful. *Breaking Through* enables people to find out what combination will work best for them.

If you are unhappy with any part of your life, making a decision to *do something* is extremely important. This book will assist each reader on the path to the correct therapist or program for what is most needed. This hopeful, optimistic book is written in a manner that will encourage every reader to begin that important journey. I also recommend *Breaking Through* to therapists everywhere, and to anyone else in the helping professions.

Ruth King, Director
The CLARE Foundation, Culver Vista, California[1]

---

[1] The CLARE Foundation is a non-profit, Los Angeles based organization supporting people's recovery through temporary residential facilities, community education, assisting other human service agencies, and offering individual recovery planning and 24 hour crisis services.

Acknowledgments

My thanks to Dr. Lee Marvin Joiner, Pat Holliday and Pat Hammond, of Human Services Institute, and to Tab Books, A Division of McGraw-Hill, Inc. for enabling me to share this effort with others.

This book became a reality with the support of the following doctors, therapists, counselors, and group leaders: Corinne Balzac, C.A.C.; Judy Bin-Nun, Ph.D.; Edward A. Dreyfus, Ph.D.; Jael Greenleaf; Amy Gross, Ph.D.; Barbara Kearney, M.A.; Ruth King; Toni Michels, Ph.D.; Donna Nelson, M.F.C.C., Nancy Rincon, M.F.C.C.; Martha Slagerman, Ph.D.; and Margaret Yates, M.D.

Additionally, my thanks to Steve Adler, Advanced Computer Services; Juliette Anthony, Dori Jackson, Bruce Preston, Sue's Secretarial Service; Ken Weston, and the Tuesday, Wednesday and Thursday women's groups.

The client and therapist names in all examples herein are fictitious. I greatly appreciate the generosity of the clients and therapists who shared their therapy experiences with me for this book.

Introduction

This book is your guide on a journey through therapy. We'll embark by helping you find the right therapist for your needs, and we'll part company as you learn when, and how, to say goodbye to your therapist. In between, you'll learn how to form a partnership with your therapist that will enable you to live a fuller, more rewarding life.

From time to time, everyone has emotional symptoms. The causes range from chronic physical pain to the emotional upsets of an unexpected loss or a lifestyle change. When the physical problem is resolved, or time heals the loss, you usually move on without difficulty. But there are times when the emotional symptoms won't go away, and you feel stuck. At these times, therapy may be your best choice.

In this book, you will learn how to save time and money by first learning what your specific needs and problems are; what makes a good therapist; and how to locate and hire the appropriate therapist for your needs.

Then you will create your own Recovery Notebook, with specific sections for the many ways you'll participate in therapy. You will learn to write down your dreams for use in therapy. You will also write about disappointments, hurtful feelings, and losses. After six months, you'll complete a comprehensive Six-Month Checkup and discuss it with your therapist to see whether the therapy partnership is working for you. You will discover that you have a strong, vibrant Inner Child who is probably eager to tell his or her story to you and to your therapist. Your Recovery Notebook will designate a special place for dialogues with that Inner Child, using innovative and successful Self-Parenting techniques.

Throughout the book, you will also find real-life examples of how others have found solutions, through therapy, to relationship problems, low self-esteem, stages of grieving, work problems, and phobias. The uses of Twelve-Step programs such as Alcoholics Anonymous, Overeaters Anonymous and Debtors Anonymous, as they work in conjunction with appropriate therapy, are fully detailed in Chapters Seven, Eight, and Nine.

You will learn what to do for yourself when your therapist goes on vacation, retires, moves away, or dies, while you are in treatment. And you will receive a checklist to help you and your therapist arrive at a mutual decision that you have completed your work in therapy.

Many clients contributed their therapy experiences to this book. May you find the trip as valuable and exciting as they did.

Section One

This section contains the symptoms or problems for which you might consider using a therapist, as well as reasons why other people have used a therapist, and how therapy has been helpful for them.

You will also discover how to eliminate possible medical reasons for your emotional difficulties. You will learn to create and use a Recovery Notebook. You will also be given a writing exercise to clarify your issues, in your own mind, before you seek therapy. These could include work or relationship problems, uncomfortable feelings such as chronic anxiety or depression, or obsessive behaviors like compulsive overeating or overspending. You will no doubt think of other issues, for consideration in therapy, once you begin to write about your feelings and your difficulties.

CHAPTER

1

Why People Use Therapy

• Why you would consider therapy • The functions of a therapist • Some limitations of therapy • Common situations in which therapy is useful • Using a Recovery Notebook

Therapy is a positive experience. Because of therapy, you will feel better, learn how to find solutions to your living problems, and become more comfortable with other people. And anything therapy cannot change, it can certainly help you to accept.

Therapy works so well because a professional therapist is trained to help you explore and understand your feelings. When you know where your feelings come from, and what they mean, you can achieve practical solutions to your living problems. Because therapy takes place in a safe and supportive atmosphere, it helps you increase your trust in your own decisions and beliefs, and you also learn to trust other people more. As a result of that trust, you will experience greater self-esteem and confidence. This increased self-esteem will result in more satisfaction everywhere, including your work life, and with your family and friends. You will have the freedom of living more fully as a result of therapy.

By talking things out with a therapist, you locate the solutions that are hidden within you. The therapists I interviewed for this book stated that people often *know* what they need to do, about many situations, but they have troubling *trusting* their own judgment. With compassionate, professional help, clients can look within to explore their own answers and then be reassured that their increasing trust in themselves is deserved.

The primary focus of this book is a look at different kinds of therapy and how they are helpful. But therapy also works well when combined with appropriate self-help programs, and with individual maintenance tools such as the writing exercises done in a Recovery Notebook. These programs and exercises are explained fully in later chapters.

SYMPTOMS

You can make good use of therapy if you have any of the following symptoms or problems:

Emotional Problems

You are anxious or restless. You are lonely or depressed. Your moods change without any warning. You feel life is not worth the effort. You are dissatisfied much of the time. You cannot control your anger. You worry about the future. You don't value your accomplishments. You feel guilty about something you did or felt.

Relationships

You hold on to angry feelings about others. You haven't recovered from a death or the breakup of a relationship. You can't get along with your parents, your spouse, your children, or your friends. You are afraid to let other people get close to you. You have trouble allowing yourself to depend on anyone else. You have questions or problems regarding sex. You repeatedly take care of others and ignore your own needs. You are overly dependent on someone else. You often feel other people are not listening to you. You don't know how to leave relationships that are not good for you.

Work Problems

You feel overwhelmed at work. You have problems with coworkers or supervisors. You have excessive tardiness or absenteeism at work. You have been terminated from several jobs. You would like a promotion, or a raise, or more training, but you're afraid to apply. You are dissatisfied with your career, but you don't know what else to do.

Thought Difficulties

You have trouble making decisions or prioritizing your time. You think about your childhood a lot. You are too preoccupied about your problems to function. You cannot remember the events of the recent past, or events from a long time ago. You have poor judgment in some living situations. You frequently do not understand what is being said to you by others.

Obsessive Behaviors

You are unable to control your drinking, drug use, compulsive spending, compulsive overeating, or other obsessive behavior. Or, perhaps, someone in your life is abusing alcohol or drugs; a compulsive overeater, a compulsive gambler or a compulsive spender; or displaying other obsessive behaviors which affect you negatively.

Phobic Disorders

You are frightened in elevators and other closed spaces. You have a fear of heights, or traveling, or flying, or being near water.

All of the above-mentioned issues can be treated successfully in therapy. The frequency of your sessions, and the length of the treatment, will depend upon your particular issues. But you do not have to have a high I.Q. or an advanced education, or even know exactly what your problem is, to participate fully in therapy.

WHAT A THERAPIST DOES

Your Therapist Will be a Partner and Helper

Together, you are going on a journey through the past, the present, and to some extent the future. This journey begins with your history. A little bit at a time, you are going to tell the story of your life and your therapist is going to "play it back" to you, in simple language, and make suggestions that will help you to grow and to change.

For example, when you go to a therapist, you may have emotions that are interfering with your ability to feel comfortable in some area of your life. Whatever you are feeling, you have a good reason. Often, these feelings are the ghosts of unresolved past hurts, and you've never told anyone about them. As you tell your story, your therapist will help you understand your history, so that it no longer intrudes on your life. Once you are able to see the original problem that caused the hurt, these ghosts from the past will cease to haunt you.

Therapy Will be a Safe Place for You

A therapist has a calm, soothing way of relating to you, from the beginning. The office is quiet and private. There are no interruptions. And, in individual therapy, there is no one in the room but you and your therapist. No one is going to argue with you about how you feel, or criticize you for anything you say. Your therapist is not going to repeat what you say to anyone else, so you can feel safe confiding anything.

You are also free, in therapy, to say *nothing* if that is how you are feeling in the beginning. Some people find this comforting if they have always felt pressure to "fill the silences" or if they are shy. You will warm up to the process as you get to know your therapist better, but if you can say "Hello," you can begin therapy work.

As therapy progresses, your trust in your therapist is sure to grow. This safe place becomes one in which you can examine intimate details about your life that you were never able to tell anyone else. Your therapist will not judge or condemn you for anything you did or said or felt. In fact, he or she will most likely remind you that you are only human. You may have confusion or guilt over issues surrounding sex, for example, because you lack basic information which your therapist will easily provide.

Your Therapist Will Help You Understand Painful Feelings

Growing pains are necessary for everyone, but sometimes it's just more comforting to feel bad *with* someone than it is to isolate. Also, the therapist's years of experience enable observation of your feelings without being threatened by them. Your anger won't be taken as a personal attack because your therapist knows that you have to express it somewhere, in order to get rid of it.

Many times, we have gone through life pushing these old, intense feelings down, which has caused us to feel anxious or depressed. A therapist is a stronger person than you are, emotionally, who is able to act as a temporary reservoir for your feelings. The therapist can be objective while you vent these feelings, and can then help you to understand them when you are calmer.

None of your powerful feelings will surprise your therapist, whose experience includes encounters with people's deepest emotions. Delving into the past, in order to change, sometimes feels uncomfortable but, because of years of experience, your therapist knows there is really nothing to fear. Your therapist can honestly reassure you that feelings have much less power over you once they are out in the open.

Your Therapist Will Help You Solve Your Living Problems

As you talk about your week's activities, your feelings, your insights, your dreams, and your interactions with other people, your therapist interprets all these details. For instance, your therapist will be able to tell you, in language that you will understand, why you may feel helpless to alter some situation in your life.

This understanding does not always solve your problem, but you will feel reassured, and even stronger, while you and your therapist sort through the problem together and arrive at a solution. This may include changing your point of view; or taking an action you hadn't thought of, that will alter the situation; or simply coming to accept the situation as it is.

Your Therapist Will Reinforce Your Best Qualities

Therapists are persons with consistency, personal integrity, and the other traits that comprise responsible, fulfilled adults. As you meet with your therapist every week, you will begin to recognize these same positive traits within yourself. Soon, you recognize these valuable qualities within yourself even when you are *not* with your therapist. This strengthens your self-esteem by letting you know you are capable of dealing with situations on your own, or that you know how and where to get assistance.

Your Therapist is There for You in Emergencies

Into every human life, there is bound to come some crisis, such as the illness or death of a loved one, for example. Your therapist will be a source of comfort to you in these times. While remaining detached enough to help you, your therapist is able to share your pain with you, so that you do not have to bear it alone. Sharing this vulnerability also allows you to feel stronger, to be more effective in your daily life during a crisis, and to help others through the situation.

Besides comforting you, your therapist is, at the same time, assessing what actions you need to take during a crisis. These actions will be explained to you; this way, you can allow yourself to feel the pain, and to move through it, while being assisted in making decisions you may not want to make alone.

Your Therapist Will Help You Through a Disappointment or a Loss

A therapist helps you to identify the losses in your life—small ones, large ones, anything that you feel sad about or need to grieve over. Grieving is a natural, human response to a loss. You may need your therapist's help to follow its course like a stream, as it makes its way through your system. Therapists are trained to help us put these losses into perspective, because not all losses share equal significance in our lives. There is more about help with losses and grieving in Chapter Ten.

Your Therapist Will Teach You to be Easier on Yourself

Because your therapist has treated you with respect every week, for example, you won't be so hard on yourself when something doesn't work out as you planned; or when you don't accomplish as much as you thought you could; or when you make an error in judgment. And this respect and kindness will transfer over to your other relationships. You'll find yourself less judgmental and more understanding of other people.

SOME LIMITATIONS OF THERAPY

Therapy is Not a Cure-All

As helpful as therapy is, for all these issues and more, it does have some limitations. For instance, therapy alone cannot cure alcoholism, drug addiction, gambling, overeating, or compulsive spending, although it can help you learn to live comfortably without the obsessive behavior. For these issues, your therapist will direct you to Alcoholics Anonymous, or to a comparable Twelve-Step program, while you are in individual therapy. When used *concurrently* with therapy, these programs offer valuable support in maintaining freedom from addiction and in reinforcing new, life-affirming living skills. There is more information about obsessive behaviors and Twelve-Step programs in Chapters Eight and Nine.

Therapy Cannot Change the Events of Your Past

The best we can *all* do about the past is to make peace with it. But therapy can change the *effects* of the past, if they are giving you trouble. In therapy you will look back, see why life was the way it was, make changes based on your therapist's experience with similar problems, and then move on to enjoy your present life. Treatment for many adult problems of childhood is covered more thoroughly in Chapter Seven.

Therapy Cannot Predict the Future

Life is what happens to each of us while we make plans. But therapy can help you set realistic goals and take appropriate measures to achieve them. A therapist cannot know *what* is going to happen to you, but a therapist is trained to help you prepare for *whatever* happens to you. This is done by first understanding, and then helping you change or eliminate, those behaviors, emotions, and beliefs that prevent you from coping effectively with your life. Your therapist will also teach you behaviors that strengthen your positive traits, thus giving you more confidence and less fear about whatever the future holds.

Therapy Cannot Change Your Entire Personality

You wouldn't want it to, anyway; if it did, then you wouldn't be you. But in therapy you will learn what traits *can't* be changed and how to adapt to them, as well as what traits *can* be changed and how to make those changes. For instance, you may be particularly sensitive to arguments or yelling but, in the past, you sat and suffered in silence. With the encouragement of a therapist, you can learn how to confront the problem, or how to walk away from the argument. Maybe you'd rather read a good book than attend a crowded party, but don't know how to say "no" to an invitation. In therapy, you will learn to do what you want to do, rather than submitting to social pressure.

WHERE THERAPY IS USEFUL

Here are some sample case studies (with names and details changed) to illustrate how therapy helps some common problems:

Growing Up in a Dysfunctional Family

Amanda was referred to therapy by her physician for her emotional problems surrounding family alcoholism. For Amanda, alcoholism on both sides of her family goes back at least four generations. Many of her relatives died of alcohol-related auto accidents, suicide, liver disease, heart disease, strokes, and mental breakdowns. As a child, she experienced sexual, physical and verbal abuse in an alcoholic home. In therapy, she was able to release appropriate feelings of anger and sadness for her damaged childhood.

Therapy was the first time Amanda had ever told anyone about the details of this painful childhood. Her therapist became her *witness to the past*, which is a vital ingredient for anyone from a dysfunctional family. Adults who were abused children often perceive the world as a fearful place because they have had no one with whom to compare their views and, in their experience, no one would listen anyway. The fear of living can be substantially reduced or eliminated when you share the details of a painful childhood with someone you trust. For this reason, there is much freedom in store in selecting a therapist as the person to hear your story. This relief is then followed up with professional treatment for the damaged childhood.

Amanda's therapist was consistent in all his behavior with her, which strengthened Amanda's trust in him, and made her feel she was worth caring about. Through her therapist's thorough history-taking, his model of consistency, his encouragement, and his reinforcement of Amanda's own abilities, much old damage was repaired and Amanda's life was reconstructed in a way that would have been impossible without therapy.

Amanda could not have done this work alone, because she needed someone to listen to her story; and then she needed someone to encourage her to take the actions that change requires. For anyone from an alcoholic or dysfunctional family, therapy is the vital link to healing and emotional freedom.

Phobic Disorders Such As the Fear of Leaving Your Home

Before therapy, if Cora went as far as the mailbox in her front yard, she hyperventilated and fainted. She was unable to hold a job, to drive a car, or to travel any distance. When she described her symptoms to her family physician, he encouraged her to participate in therapy for the treatment of this problem.

Her early therapy consisted of one weekly appointment, and taking short walks alone every day, at a distance she and her therapist predetermined. She was encouraged by her therapist to go only as far from home as she felt she could comfortably manage. Farther along in her therapy, Cora felt confident enough to extend her emotional comfort zone by walking a little farther, and by learning to drive. She was eventually able to hold a job, keep social engagements, and take vacations.

Cora's therapist worked at Cora's pace, and he didn't push her too quickly, because he was experienced in the use of *behavior modification therapy*. But he firmly encouraged her to stretch her comfort zone while they explored, together, possible causes for her anxiety. With therapy, her *agoraphobia* was greatly improved, and she has been given tools to deal with it, should it recur.

When Couples Disagree

A problem regarding their upcoming wedding brought Lois and Tim to counseling. By themselves, they had been able to resolve all the major issues confronting most engaged couples except one: where to live. They had met and become engaged in Seattle, where Lois and her family lived and where she intended to remain. Tim had recently been offered a better career position in Dallas, where he wanted to relocate. They entered therapy together, determined to resolve the issue or break the engagement.

Their therapist suggested that Lois make a list of the reasons she did not wish to move from Seattle, and that Tim make a list of the reasons he felt he had to take the job in Dallas. Then she asked Lois and Tim to trade lists and each defend the opposite position. They were both able to see the other's point of view; in this way, their therapist demonstrated how rigidly both of them had clung to the need to "win." She suggested that this need had become more important, in the anxiety of the wedding, than their original commitment to one another.

It became clear to Lois and Tim, rather rapidly, that they could happily live and work in either location. They decided to move to Dallas, in the interest of Tim's career, on a one-year trial basis, to be reevaluated at the end of that year. During their stay in Dallas, Lois has visited her family in Seattle one week a month.

Because of their therapy together before their marriage, Lois and Tim were able to be more vigilant about their need to "be right" when it surfaced later on, and to deal with it immediately. They are both active people, committed to a variety of interests, so much effective "list trading" still goes on in their home.

Recovering From a Loss

Robert began seeing a therapist following a tragic auto accident that claimed the life of his 27-year-old wife. Left alone with two small children to raise, Robert felt angry, bereft and bewildered. He had only short-term help from his retired parents and in-laws during this time, and Robert felt overwhelmed. He became temporarily unable to think clearly, to set daily priorities, or to look at his two small children without crying.

Robert's therapist provided essential support in the early stages of his readjustment. She referred Robert to a grief workshop where he was able to share his feelings with understanding people who had also lost someone. And she helped Robert redefine his children's immediate and long-term needs, as well as his own. Robert's therapist recommended that both children be seen by a child psychologist, in order to work through their grief for their lost mother. Although not fully recovered from this loss,

Robert is back at work and his children are back in school. Supportive therapy has enabled this family to get on with the business of living.

Evaluating Your Achievements and Giving Up Illusions

Thomas, a widower, entered therapy due to depression following his sixtieth birthday. In therapy, he learned how to make peace with his past achievements, and how to say goodbye to his boyhood dreams. Over the course of his treatment he was able to accept that, although he was not going to become an airline pilot, he had enjoyed a fulfilling career as an aeronautical engineer.

When Thomas' sons were young, he had not spent as much time with them as he would have liked, because of his work. He told his therapist he was concerned that he had not been a good parent. But, as his therapist encouraged him to speak of his sons, Thomas realized that he had been there for both boys, as young adults, when they had needed financial assistance and career guidance. With his therapist's encouragement, Thomas also became more actively involved with his beloved grandchildren, an activity which he enjoyed and which strengthened his bond to his sons.

For Thomas, therapy provided an effective look over his shoulder at his past, with more satisfaction than sadness, regarding both his professional life and his role as a parent. With his therapist, Thomas also discussed and rejected many of the myths of aging, so he awakens to each new day with more enthusiasm than depression.

Treating the Entire Family Together

Roberta and Clark pursued family therapy because they felt their teenage son, Richie, was withdrawing from them. They could both see the gradual disintegration of Richie's values and his increased lack of interest in life. But they felt unable to talk to him or to help him.

In family therapy, Roberta and Clark were able to confront Richie with their feelings of disappointment and confusion concerning his behavior. Richie was able to respond at first with only silence and sullen stares. He felt he was there "so you can all pick on me." The therapist gained Richie's confidence, however, by consistently acknowledging Richie's words and feelings, whatever they were. She did not criticize what Richie said, or discount his presence in any way.

Soon, Richie sensed the therapist was willing to work patiently, as long as it took, to help him solve his problems. As the therapist drew him out, and as he continued to meet with his parents and the therapist weekly, Richie began to reveal the feelings of fear and inadequacy that lay beneath his initial hostility. Richie felt considerable pressure to abuse drugs and alcohol, as many of his peers were doing, but he had been unable to confide this to his parents in the past.

Now, although Richie's feelings were emerging, family communication problems remained to be solved. For this, the family therapist introduced them all to helpful skills they could use at home, when talking about intense, emotional issues. As the family therapy progressed still further, Richie regained his enthusiasm for life. He had the support of both the therapist and his parents in remaining drug free; and he formed new, appropriate friendships. He developed inner self-confidence; and he took many suggestions from his therapist, regarding his appearance and attitude, that his parents were still learning how to communicate to him.

Although their home is not one hundred percent peaceful, the daily battles of this family have ceased, and the battleground has been moved, when necessary, from their living room to the therapist's office.

Temporary Substitute for a Spouse or Partner

Isobel sought grief counseling when her husband of forty years died, after a lingering illness. When her grieving was completed, however, she experienced some reluctance to terminate her therapy sessions. This confused her; she had grieved and gotten on with the business of living, so why stay? Together, she and her therapist made a list of possible reasons why Isobel felt she needed to remain in weekly therapy at this time in her life.

What they discovered, together, was that for forty years Isobel had been used to sharing the details of her day, across the dinner table, with a partner who was now deceased. Her three grown children were attentive, when they could make the time, but they seemed ambivalent to meeting Isobel's need for regular companionship. Although she had resumed a full life, Isobel's need for a partner remained unmet.

In her therapist, Isobel found a valuable and comforting listener until she could form new ties. She says her therapy sessions gave her a feeling of independence, and someone in whom to confide. She is enthusiastic about her life and, with her therapist's encouragement, she has made new friends since her husband's death. She feels less needy, and the time she spends with her grown children is more rewarding to her than ever.

Using a therapist proved to be beneficial in providing these clients with a safe place to examine their feelings; to practice new ways of communicating with family members; to make difficult decisions; to lean temporarily on a stronger person until a crisis had passed; and to surrender old illusions in order to confront the facts of life. Many more uses for a therapist will be discussed in later chapters.

USING A RECOVERY NOTEBOOK

It will be helpful to create your own Recovery Notebook. Divide a loose-leaf binder into the following sections for writing exercises and for recording information. Each section will be discussed, in detail, later in this book.

My Medical History

You may wish to record medical information about yourself, which you obtain in your physical examination. This section of your notebook is also a handy place for answering the questions listed on page 31, if you need further medical treatment.

Why I Want to See a Therapist

Once you rule out any medical causes for your emotional or living problems, it will help you and your therapist to be as clear as possible about your reasons for seeking therapy. You will be writing down these reasons in this section of your Recovery Notebook, and taking them to your first therapy appointment.

My Life's Goals

Having some idea of your ambitions concerning family, work life, education, and hobbies helps your therapist get to know you. You will be noting these goals in this section of your Recovery Notebook, and reading these goals to your therapist.

My Wildest Fantasies

Your fantasies tell you a lot about what you really want from life. Your therapist can help you understand yourself better if you share the content of some of your recurring daydreams. You will be writing down these fantasies in this section of your Recovery Notebook.

My First Impressions of Therapy

In this section, you will be writing about anything you observed, or thought, or felt during your first appointment with your therapist. This information will play a role for you in your Six-Month Checkup with your therapist.

My Observations

Sometimes, during the course of therapy, you will have insights about yourself that you didn't realize before. This new way of looking at your life, at other people, and at yourself, will be developing because the therapy is working well. That is one of the positive changes your therapist is expecting from the treatment, and it helps to hear about these observations.

My Secrets and Resentments

Holding on to secrets or resentments, such as old anger or a disappointment from the past, makes it difficult for you to get other work done in therapy, because the secret or resentment becomes your primary focus. When your mind is busy *not* telling your therapist a secret, or *staying* resentful, you can't concentrate on therapy. You will learn writing exercises in later chapters to help you process these secrets and resentments.

My Dreams

Your dreams provide your therapist with helpful information about your unconscious conflicts and how to resolve them. If you write down your dreams, as best you can recall them, and then read them to your therapist, you both have the opportunity to evaluate the messages your subconscious is sending you while you sleep.

My Therapy Payments and Insurance Records

Your Recovery Notebook is a handy place to record your therapy payments and insurance information. Taking responsibility for this part of your therapy will increase your ability to depend on yourself, while providing you with current payment and insurance information.

Suggestions From My Therapist

From time to time, your therapist will make suggestions to you about different ways of looking at your life. You may also be given recommendations for dealing with a situation or a person differently than you had considered. But you can only follow that guidance if you can remember what was said. Taking your Recovery Notebook to your appointments and jotting down your therapist's recommendations is helpful.

Messages From My Inner Child

In Chapter Seven you will learn about some of the latest techniques for repairing emotional damage from a dysfunctional family. In this section of your Recovery Notebook you will be encouraged to begin and maintain a dialogue with your own Inner Child, in order to become a more effective and comfortable adult.

Completing the Past

In Chapter Ten you will learn how your life's losses affect you, why they linger, and why grief transforms loss into inner strength. You can use this section of your Recovery Notebook, for example, to write letters to people you cannot contact in person, in order to feel complete about your relationship with them. For this purpose, a format and sample letter are offered in Chapter Ten.

My Six-Month Checkup

This section of your notebook will be used to record your answers to the suggested questions listed on pages 75, 76 and 77 for charting your progress in therapy.

My Termination

The final section of your Recovery Notebook will be reserved for your responses to those questions on pages 145 and 146, regarding your termination from therapy.

Some of the other issues covered in later chapters include:

- how to find an appropriate therapist for yourself;

- how the process of therapy works;

- learning what is responsible therapy behavior on your therapist's part and yours;

- how to tell whether therapy is really working for you after six months;

- what to do when your therapist goes on vacation;

- how to discuss your termination from therapy and what that process is like; and,

- where to obtain information about free Twelve-Step programs all over the country for alcoholism, eating, disorders and compulsive spending.

CHAPTER

2

Before You Seek Therapy

• How your body and your emotions work together • Physical exercise—an important tool • PMS and menopause can create emotional symptoms • Aging doesn't mean you have to sing the blues • Physical pain has a message for you • A writing tool to help clarify your reasons for seeking therapy.

PASSING THE PHYSICAL

Sometimes our emotions are expressed quite graphically through our bodies. These statements may sound familiar:

"You make me sick!"
"You're a pain in the neck!"
"I can't stomach this any longer!"
"I'm so angry I can't see straight!"
"This breaks my heart."

By adulthood, we have frequently learned to interpret these physical messages and to confront the emotional distress directly, in which case the physical symptoms soon disappear.

On the other hand, it is often true that some physical problem is causing you to feel irritable or depressed. When the physical problem is resolved, the emotional symptoms often disappear as well.

Therapists recommend that you begin by combing through your physical system for the culprit before you seek therapy. According to medical experts, the early detection and cure of many physical illnesses begins with tracing your emotions to their physical cause.

To rule out any physical causes for your emotional discomfort before you consult a therapist, it will help you to have a thorough medical examination by your family physician. Such an examination will tell your doctor whether some physical problem is causing you to have emotional symptoms. This exam, for instance, might include tests to see whether low blood sugar, or some cardiac irregularity, could be making you feel anxious. Your doctor will know, after hearing you describe your emotional discomfort, exactly what tests to administer, and how to resolve any physical problems. Although it sounds like a lot, you'll feel relieved, after this exam, knowing that you've taken the first step toward eliminating your discomfort.

When your examination is finished, speak with your physician regarding an explanation of all the results. If your cholesterol level is high, find out why. There may be something you can do about it in your daily living, such as taking more physical exercise, or reducing saturated fats in your diet. Know when your test results fall within the expected normal range; when they do not, and what you can do about that. If you suffer from hypertension, or your doctor mentions that any of your test results indicate medical treatment, including medication, be sure you understand what the suggested treatment plan is and then follow it.

Vitamins and Minerals

Most of us require some assistance in selecting vitamins and nutritional supplements because there are many such products available. Even if we regularly maintain a sensible diet, we still may not consume the minimum daily requirements of some vitamins. Ask your physician's recommendations about vitamins for someone your age, in your physical condition, with your lifestyle.

It is *not* recommended that you self-prescribe vitamins or nutritional supplements, unless you have discussed this with your doctor. These over-the-counter products are intended to be taken as part of your overall health plan, with medical approval and supervision, because they are just as potent as prescription medications, in come cases.

Pharmacists also deal frequently with the manufacturers and distributors of these products, and keep up-to-date with the proper dosage and any side effects of the vitamins and nutrients they provide for your purchase. Pharmacists can be excellent guides to the world of vitamins and nutrients, in conjunction with your physician's approval of their use.

THE VALUE OF EXERCISE

According to the American Heart Association, most Americans don't exercise enough. Many of us also have sedentary occupations that cause or aggravate heart disease, hypertension, obesity, depression, restlessness, and fatigue.

Exercise improves the power and tone of the muscles. It helps the blood by increasing the amount of oxygen that is carried by the red blood cells. It stimulates the circulation, making certain that tissues receive the proper amounts of oxygen. Your heart, lungs, and digestive system will thank you for exercising.

And there is an emotional payoff for regular exercise. One of the benefits is reduced tension and an increased sense of well-being. When you exercise vigorously, your brain activates chemical substances known as *endorphins* that produce heightened feelings of well-being. That's why it is not unusual to experience a naturally induced sense of pleasure following your exercise. For this reason, exercise is often medically recommended as a part of the treatment plan for depression.

If you can't bring yourself to participate in some other form of exercise, park several blocks from your destination and take a brisk walk. This requires no fancy clothing, special training, gym membership, or exercise equipment; and it's free!

Try to become aware of your own rhythm as you walk. Start by warming up at home; sway, stretch, and bend until you find a pace that feels comfortable, and familiar. Tune in to your body's natural motion. Observe your heartbeat, your breathing, and your balance. Soon, you'll find a natural walking rhythm that produces more energy, improved concentration, and heightened mental focus.

PMS, MENOPAUSE, AND EMOTIONS

If you're a woman, you may have emotional symptoms commonly associated with either pre-menstrual syndrome (PMS) or menopause, which can be relieved with properly prescribed estrogen or hormone replacement therapy. Ask your physician to check your hormone count, and to discuss it with you, when you undergo your regular gynecologic examination.

Common complaints associated with pre-menstrual syndrome include irritability, depression, and headaches. These symptoms usually abate after menstruation begins but, unless you chart your own cycle, they can easily be misdiagnosed as deep psychological disturbances requiring unnecessary therapy.

Somewhere between about age forty-five and fifty, the average woman begins to experience symptoms of menopause. Most common is the appearance of hot flashes, which cause the entire body to become warm. There is often excessive perspiration followed by chills. Frequently present, also, are palpitations, headaches, dizziness, irritability, uncontrollable tearfulness, mood swings, and sleeplessness.

Effective in treating these symptoms are estrogenic hormones but, like PMS, unless you are armed with information about menopause, the emotional mood swings can become severe enough to alarm you, or cause you to enter therapy prematurely. If you are in this age range, and you are experiencing any of these symptoms, you need, first, to obtain a gynecological examination, before seeking therapy.

IT'S NEVER TOO LATE

We're never too young to begin solid health care habits, and we're also never too old. Men and women over the age of fifty are the biggest consumers of health care in this country. As a society, we are living longer. No matter how late you begin them, the simple health care guidelines noted below can have a significant, positive impact on the length and quality of your life. They enable you to savor the years after fifty, instead of just surviving. In many instances, these simple directions also eliminate your need for therapy by increasing your feelings of well-being and ridding you of minor emotional complaints.

Eat Right!

A well-balanced diet is a foundation for lifelong health. Unless your physician has recommended different guidelines, experts now believe that fat should make up no more than 30 percent of our total caloric intake. Whole grains, legumes, and fruits and vegetables are recommended sources of fiber. And a watchful eye on your daily intake of sodium (salt) is an excellent idea.

Get Moving!

It is important to note that exercise does not have to be aerobic to be beneficial. Fitness is not limited to the young. Any movement that increases flexibility, endurance, and strength will also alleviate joint stiffness, back pain, headaches, and a variety of other symptoms associated with aging, including depression.

Stop Smoking!

Smoking increases your risk of developing cancer, emphysema, and heart disease. Many older smokers become discouraged and believe it's too late to stop. But the American Cancer Society notes that, when you stop smoking, health benefits always begin at once, lessening your chances of contracting cancer and coronary heart disease.

Nicotine is a powerful drug which can cause irritability, depression, sleep disorders and loss of appetite. Becoming a nonsmoker can improve your emotional well-being soon after quitting. Also, people are becoming more sensitive to the adverse health effects of secondhand smoke and this can lead to conflicts in the smoker's relationships.

Acute and Chronic Pain, and What They Tell You

According to physicians, physical pain is our most common national health complaint. *Acute* pain comes on suddenly, is very intense or intolerable, and often subsides quickly. Persistent, acute pain, with or without other symptoms, should signal you to consult your medical doctor immediately. You will be helped more effectively if you can be specific in describing your pain. If possible, before you see your doctor, answer the following questions in your Recovery Notebook, and take the questions and answers with you to your appointment:

• When did your pain start and where is it located?
• Did you injure yourself, or is there another obvious cause for the pain?
• Is the pain constant or intermittent?
• Do some body positions or activities either reduce the pain or aggravate it?
• Are you taking any prescription medications?
• What are they called?
• If possible, take your prescription container with you.
• Do you have any other symptoms such as vomiting, dizziness, fainting, or bleeding?

About one-third of Americans suffer some kind of *chronic* and often disabling pain. Chronic physical pain is an alarm your body sounds when something is wrong. As well as being a warning, it also makes most of us crabby. If chronic pain is untreated, it can eventually create such symptoms as irritability, fatigue, anxiety, and depression.

If you suffer from incurable chronic pain, a chronic pain management program may provide relief. Included in such a program are physical therapy; stretching exercises; occupational therapy for accomplishing everyday tasks without worsening the pain; and relaxation techniques and deep breathing exercises to break the pain - stress cycle.

Most major hospitals or your family doctor can refer you to a chronic pain management program. There are few experiences more discouraging and draining than chronic physical pain. Don't suffer in silence, if learning pain management techniques may eliminate some of your emotional symptoms.

After ruling out any physical causes for your emotional difficulties, it will help you to be clear about the reasons why you want to consult a therapist. We don't always have time, in our busy lives, to settle down comfortably and get in touch with our feelings and our emotional needs. Take the time now to clarify, in writing, your reasons for considering therapy. In the process of doing this writing, you might find you have some of your own solutions already!

Find a quiet place where you may be alone. In your Recovery Notebook, make a list of the things that are bothering you. Don't go back and edit this list for professional eyes; you aren't going to publish it. Leave it the way you write it down. Whatever is bothering you, you need to be as specific and honest about it as possible, with yourself and also with your therapist. This honesty usually comes through in your first, spontaneous notes.

Don't read this list to your spouse, mother, sister, children, or friends, because everybody will have a different opinion. Just share it with your therapist at your first appointment and keep it for reference. You will also be using this writing in the Six Month Checkup described in Chapter Six.

The chances are pretty good that you already know something about what is wrong. You may have tried several solutions to a living problem, for example. You may know why they didn't work, but you still have the problem and you don't know what to try next. Your therapist will help you identify why you are stuck and help you move on, one step at a time.

Also make a list of your life goals, even if you think you cannot achieve them. These would include short-term and long-term educational, career, and family plans. They will be addressed in your therapy, and you will evaluate their progress in your Six-Month Checkup.

Finally, list your ongoing fantasies and daydreams. These are things you'd do, for instance, if money were no object and you were free to go anywhere and do anything you wished. This list will play an additional role in your Six-Month Checkup.

CHAPTER
3
Therapists and Therapy -
Practitioners and Methodology

• *The training and skills of different kinds of therapists* •
Some therapy methods • *Step one—your mental health
evaluation* • *What therapists have in common.*

All therapists have certain skills and training in common.
For instance, they are able to recognize the symptoms of
a variety of mental illnesses and emotional difficulties.
They understand how various symptoms have developed
in individual clients. They possess a solid, working know-
ledge of the mind's organization and its functions. They
can assess how a person's mental and emotional defenses
work. They know how people react to loss and to stress.
And they can interpret how someone's thoughts, behaviors,
and feelings interact, to form that individual's personality.

The goal of all therapists is to help you understand what
is troubling you and what you can do about it. What varies

is their training and their approach to the problem. Here are descriptions of several different kinds of therapists and several different kinds of treatment.

PRACTITIONERS

Psychiatrist

There's a very old joke, almost universal among medical students, that goes like this:

A psychiatrist knows *nothing* and does nothing.
An internist knows *everything* and does nothing.
A surgeon knows nothing and does *everything*.
And a coroner knows everything *and* does everything, but he is very, very late.

In the case of the psychiatrist, at least, the joke is untrue. A psychiatrist is a doctor with a medical degree, who studies and treats human emotions. Psychiatrists attend medical school and then perform a three-year internship, followed by a three-year residency in a teaching hospital. They perform diagnostic procedures and are able to prescribe medications. Sometimes a form of therapy called psychoanalysis is used (see below), and sometimes other forms of therapy, including hypnosis. A psychiatrist is usually the overall manager of cases in a psychiatric hospital, a psychiatric ward of a medical hospital, or a chemical dependency unit.

When one of their clients is hospitalized, psychiatrists receive much assistance from social workers, occupational therapists, psychiatric nurses and technicians, and dance and art therapists. These people are called a treatment team. When you enter a hospital for psychiatric purposes, this team joins together to help you recover from an emotional or mental illness.

Psychologist

Psychologists are non-medical practitioners who attend five years of graduate school after college. They perform one year of internship during graduate school, and one year afterwards, usually in a clinic or a hospital. They study research and conduct a major research project to earn a Ph.D. Psychologists are not permitted to prescribe medications because they did not attend medical school. However, if you are in treatment with a psychologist who feels you require medication as part of your therapy, you will be referred to a psychiatrist for further evaluation and monitoring of the medication. Clinical psychologists and psychiatrists often work together in the treatment of emotional and mental illnesses, treating clients on both an inpatient and an outpatient basis.

Social Worker

Social workers attend two years of graduate school after college, followed by two years of field work in community agencies, family agencies or hospitals. Social workers then perform individual and group therapy, and often specialize in family therapy.

Psychoanalyst

Psychoanalysts receive five years of training following medical school, or following a degree as a psychologist or social worker. Most psychoanalysts are medical doctors but, currently, many well-qualified psychologists and social workers are also being graduated as psychoanalysts from analytic training institutes throughout the country.

Alcoholism Counselor

These counselors are often either recovering alcoholics themselves, or they are from alcoholic families. College level education and training in addictions, counseling, and psychology are required for certification in Alcohol and Drug Abuse Counseling.

METHODOLOGY

Biofeedback

Biofeedback is a technique that teaches you how to control a specific function in your body. Let's pretend you have high blood pressure as the result of your reaction to stress (although I hope you don't). An expert technician in biofeedback will examine and evaluate you, and then introduce you to the techniques of biofeedback, which you will practice at home. These techniques will include learning how to send verbal messages to your subconscious, designed to eliminate the excessive stress reactions which have caused your elevated blood pressure.

First, you will meet with this technician in a goal-setting session to establish what you want to accomplish with biofeedback (in our example, lowering your high blood pressure). Then you will see this technician on a once-a-week basis for about a month. You will have several termination treatments and follow-up sessions. The time period for this training should take no longer than three to four months (10 to 12 treatments), and significant improvement has been shown in less than three months.

The Menninger Foundation in Kansas developed a program in which clients practiced biofeedback techniques for fifteen minutes, four to seven times each day, in a successful effort to rid themselves of migraine headaches. If you are well-motivated, you may find this tool valuable in altering your responses to stress. If your family physician feels it would improve your situation, he or she can recommend a licensed biofeedback technician.

Individual Therapy

In individual therapy, you are the only client in treatment during a session with your therapist. You and your therapist meet once a week, or sometimes more often, depending upon your issues. You discuss whatever is going on in your life, as well as your feelings, your beliefs, and your thoughts. You examine your relationships at home, with family, and at work, and learn ways they can be improved. In individual therapy, the focus is always on you and how your life can be made better.

Individual therapy can be performed by a social worker, a psychologist, or a psychiatrist. If your issues revolve around alcoholism, drug addiction, or other compulsive behavior, a certified Alcoholism Counselor may be helpful.

Psychoanalysis

Psychoanalysis is both a *theory* about how therapy should work, and a *treatment method*. Here are several definitions as given by various practitioners:

- Psychoanalysis is a theory of the psychology of human development and behavior.
- It is a method of research, and a system of therapy, originating with Sigmund Freud.
- It is a way of tracing your current emotions and your everyday behavior, through free association and dream analysis, to the *unconscious* part of your mind.

In psychoanalysis, you usually go to therapy three to five times a week. The psychoanalyst often says very little but is working silently and unobtrusively, on several levels at one time, to interpret what you say. You are encouraged to associate freely and spontaneously about anything that comes into your mind, and also to describe your dreams.

This free association allows you and your psychoanalyst to determine what areas of your life you feel conflicted about. You learn how that conflict is currently expressed by you in undesirable or self-destructive ways. You explore constructive alternatives for processing and expressing those conflicts, leading to a more satisfying way of life for you. A complete psychoanalysis takes several years but, for people interested in much self-exploration, it can be a thorough means of uncovering and repairing the unconscious conflicts which have caused them trouble.

Group Therapy

In this form of treatment, the therapist can observe firsthand how you behave in relationships with other people. Individual therapy is really limited to your side of the story, since no one else is in the room except you and the therapist. But in group, you soon come to behave pretty much as you do with other people everywhere, so much value is derived from this setting.

You may be in group therapy and individual therapy simultaneously with the same therapist, if your therapist advises it and you agree that it sounds worthwhile. Group members may all enter a group at once, or a new client may enter an "open" group. In an open group, a client who drops out is replaced by another; the group continues indefinitely.

In the getting-acquainted stage, as you each tell a little of your story, you learn how the other group members react and respond to your behavior. You come to modify or give up certain actions, or ways of dealing with others, as you see that they are ineffective. And you learn, from the other group members, ways of relating that you can try out in your own life. Some of these new techniques will work for you and some may not. But your participation in group therapy creates many new solutions for you to test.

Once you get over your "newcomer shyness," the meetings take on a sense of belonging. You begin to see your fellow group members as associates, instead of merely as people with whom to work out old issues. Sometimes, because you have shared powerful emotions and much healing together, nurturing relationships are formed which continue beyond your time spent together in the group therapy setting.

Marital Therapy

This form of therapy helps couples with marriage and family issues. One common issue for which couples enter marital therapy is relating to one another intimately and sustaining this intimacy over a long period of time. Many couples bring intense feelings and old beliefs to a marriage. Therapy helps both partners to separate emotional overreactions and outdated ideas from necessary and practical decisions such as: who will keep the family financial records and pay the bills? Who does the bulk of the housekeeping, or is it shared equally? Who has primary child care responsibility?

In marital therapy, couples may also learn to make decisions about continuing education, job changes, and retirement. They can learn to handle in-law difficulties and cope with the catastrophic illness or death of a parent. When grown children leave home, a couple may need help adjusting to one another again. And many couples seek help for sexual difficulties such as infidelity, impotency, infertility, and frigidity.

Marital therapy is also utilized by couples who are *planning* to be married, as we saw in Chapter Two with Lois and Tim. Even if you have no serious conflicts as an engaged couple, doubts often arise once the wedding date is etched on the invitations. Couples with apprehensions and normal reservations about marriage often experience a tremendous amount of relief, from marital therapy.

Family Therapy

This is a convenient way for the therapist to see your whole family at one time. It is effective because the problems that members of the family have with one another become readily apparent when the family is seen together. As with Roberta, David, and their son Richie, who we met in Chapter Two, family therapy also results in improved communication among all members.

Other issues for which families enter therapy as a unit might be: how to make difficult major decisions affecting the entire family, or how to divide the various household and financial responsibilities of family members. Dealing with the changing needs of the family, as children are born and as children grow older, and resolving sibling rivalry among children, can also be dealt with in family therapy. Finally, this type of therapy can provide a forum for airing complaints and arriving at compromises regarding how family members spend their time; and designing ways for the family to spend quality time together.

STEP ONE
Your Mental Health Evaluation

If you are not certain what type of therapy to pursue, your family physician can help you make arrangements for a mental health evaluation. This evaluation is performed by a psychiatrist or a psychologist for the purpose of determining whether therapy would benefit you and, if so, what treatment is best for your needs. A mental health evaluation can be useful but costly, so be sure you discuss the fee with your doctor in advance. You may also wish to call your insurance company representative to see if this assessment is covered by your health insurance policy.

The mental health evaluation will include an interview between you and the evaluator and, possibly, some psychological testing. Additionally, the evaluator will review any medical records provided by your physician.

Taking Down Your History

In your mental health evaluation, the therapist will ask you for information such as the following:

- how you are feeling now, physically and emotionally;
- whether you have a history of emotional problems; physical illnesses, surgeries, or serious accidents;
- whether you smoke; use alcohol; drink coffee; or have ever used drugs;
- whether you are currently taking any medications, including pain killers, birth control pills, or large quantities of vitamins;
- where you went to school;
- where you have worked;
- if you have been in the military service;
- where you were born and raised;
- your parents' background;
- how many children were in your family;
- what your childhood was like;
- whether you are single, married, widowed, separated, or divorced;
- information about your spouse and your children, such as their ages and any illness or problems they have;

- what your current social life is like; and,
- what hobbies or recreational activities you prefer.

This part of your evaluation is known as a mental health history, and your responses will become part of the medical records available to your therapist.

Psychological Testing

As a part of your mental health evaluation, you may be asked to undergo some psychological testing. Perhaps the most familiar of these is the *Rorschach Ink Blot Test*, which involves cards with ink blots that look like whatever you *think* they look like. From your answers, the evaluator can tell more about what you are feeling and thinking. It is helpful to know that there is no way to get an "A" or to "fail" a psychological test. The responses you give on a psychological test merely measure the level of difficulty you are having in specific areas, and help your new therapist learn more about you.

Psychological tests also help the evaluator to assess whether you can concentrate and be attentive, or whether you are distracted or preoccupied. Your anxiety or depression levels and your intelligence range can be measured, and the evaluator can determine whether you have any memory problems. These test results can also be provided to your new therapist, to give that person a better feeling for what your issues will be.

A thorough mental health evaluation, including history taking, interview, and psychological testing, can often save time and expense in steering you in the direction of an appropriate therapist.

Section Two

This section of the book will tell you what qualities to look for in a therapist, and what referral sources are most helpful.

You will also see how therapy sessions actually work, what is expected of you, what your first appointment accomplishes, and how the relationship develops between you and your therapist.

Use of your Recovery Notebook will be further explained in this section. You will be given writing tools to record and report your dreams, secrets, and resentments; tips to make your therapist's vacation easier on you; a simple relaxation technique for stress reduction; and a Six-Month Checkup guide to help you chart your progress in therapy.

4

A Competent Therapist
and How to Find One

• *The critical Four C's: credentials, communication, consistency, and compassion* • *Referrals from friends and physicians* • *Fees, appointments, and insurance*

THE FOUR C's

Credentials

After receiving the appropriate education, a person must then obtain a license to be a therapist. The requirements governing these licenses are mandated at the state governmental level and they vary from state to state. In California, the licenses are awarded as follows:

Child Counselors, Clinical Social Workers, Marriage and Family Counselors, and Psychologists are licensed by the state *Board of Behavioral Science Examiners* and their licenses are issued through the state Department of Consumer Affairs.

Clinical Psychologists and Psychiatrists are licensed by the *Board of Medical Quality Assurance* and their licenses are issued through the state Department of Consumer Affairs.

Periodically, therapists undergo either a written exam or an oral exam, in order to renew these licenses.

If a therapist is employed by a governmental agency, or by a private mental health facility, including detoxification centers, their employer provides for their malpractice insurance. If a therapist is a private practitioner, they provide their own malpractice insurance.

Three other qualities that comprise a competent therapist are the elements of communication skills, consistency in the therapeutic relationship, and a great deal of compassion.

Communication

A good therapist is an experienced communicator; that means actively *listening* to you. The focus of therapy is on you and on the content of your session; a good therapist is not distracted from that task. From this active listening, a therapist is able to determine what your difficulties are, and what solutions can be offered to you. A good therapist pays close attention to what is taking place in your sessions.

Being a good communicator also means the therapist knows how to *talk* to you. Only language that you understand will be used, and nothing that is said by either of you will be skipped over before you fully understand it. Your therapist will also be teaching you new and more effective ways of talking to other people in your life as your therapy progresses.

Consistency

A good therapist is consistent, and shows it by opening the door to the waiting room on time for each appointment and ending each session at the same time. A therapist's mood is consistent from one week to the next. Because a good therapist knows the importance of staying current with his or her own life, the focus in your session is on you.

A good therapist is also consistently able to empathize with your deepest emotions and to help you to understand them. And being around your therapist will help you develop the quality of consistency within yourself, so you will know that you can rely upon yourself and your judgment.

Compassion

Another important quality is compassion. Compassion is what allows a therapist to relate to your pain, your losses, your grief, and the other characteristics that make you human. Compassion is a quality in a therapist that you can't evaluate as easily as credentials, fees, or a convenient address. But people who become therapists truly want to help their clients, and the quality of compassion within them is the reason.

Compassion is a quality you will sense and appreciate as you get to know your therapist better. As you go along, you will find your therapist allowing you to express your anger and hurt feelings without interruption. Your therapist will agree with you that life is hard, when life is hard, and will be willing to wait it out with you when you grieve a loss. And, always, your therapist will be kind to you and will be there next week.

In summary, the Four C's that *must* shine through in a competent therapist are credentials, communication, consistency, and compassion. If you re-read this section periodically, you will begin to know how your therapist is measuring up to these standards, but be assured that most measure up quite well.

Regarding whether to select a man or a woman as your therapist, many people have worked with therapists of both sexes and found it affected the results very little if at all. However, if you have any concerns about this question, it would help to address them with your therapist in your first session. If you have no preference about whether you work with a man or a woman, follow your hunch and go with the therapist you think you will like best.

HOW TO FIND A COMPETENT THERAPIST

In seeking a therapist, a recommendation from someone you know is a practical option and a good beginning. If you have a relative or a friend who is in therapy, ask that person to share with you, in a general way, how therapy is helping and how he or she feels about the therapist. Take into consideration the guidelines noted above, as you listen to your friend's experience.

If this therapist sounds like someone in whom you could confide, then call for an appointment. If it doesn't work out, your source is no more to blame than if the recommendation had been for a restaurant at which you suffer through a mediocre steak dinner. Keep searching.

Another good source is your family physician, who may know a mental health associate to whom you can be referred. But be as specific as possible about the *nature* of your problems, because there are nearly as many specialties these days as there are therapists. These specialties include help for marital and relationship problems, help for adults from dysfunctional families, help with your children and their behavior problems, help for alcoholism and compulsive disorders, and grief counseling, for instance. Your doctor will want to refer you to the appropriate therapist, so give him or her as much information as possible. If you are comfortable doing so, it will be helpful to read to your doctor your reasons for seeking a therapist, from your Recovery Notebook.

If you are active in your church, pastoral counseling with your minister, priest, or rabbi may be an avenue you wish to pursue. Clergymen are well-trained in dealing with the living problems of their parishioners, and you will have the added advantage of speaking candidly with someone you already know. If you feel you require individual, marital, or family therapy, your church pastor may also be helpful in referring you to a therapist.

Major hospitals have access to information regarding therapists who specialize in various forms of treatment. When you call, ask for their *Physician Referral Service.* Someone in that department will assess your requirements and then recommend several therapists from whom you may select candidates. If you have some ideas about what is troubling you, ask these candidates whether they honestly feel they could be helpful in that area. This is the only way you can really know in advance if someone's specific area of expertise matches up with your particular needs.

FEES

When you call to make an appointment with a therapist, ask about the fees. If you can't afford this therapist's fee, you may wish to inquire about a one-time consultation charge. In that instance, the therapist would see you one time, learn as much about you as possible, and then refer you to an associate whose fee you can afford. Most therapists are generous in making time to do such a consultation.

What your therapy is going to cost you will be partly determined by what you can afford to pay. Therapists set their fees by what is currently being charged by most therapists in their area of the country. Most therapy sessions last for fifty minutes and, in California, the fee for such a session ranges from $60.00 to $125.00 at the time of the writing of this book. The lower end of this range is generally charged by alcoholism counselors, social workers, marriage and family counselors, and psychologists. The high end of the range is generally the fee for clinical psychologists, inpatient care with a psychiatrist, often including medication supervision, and for outpatient fol-low-up visits after a psychiatric hospitalization.

In the final analysis, you will have to decide, after a reasonable length of time, if you feel you are being charged an appropriate fee for your therapy. But before you ever enter therapy, you are certainly free to telephone several therapists in your area, and ask about their current fees. Most are used to this kind of inquiry and realize it is the only way for consumers to determine what is the "going rate" for therapy.

Once you enter therapy, always notify your therapist if you cannot keep your appointment. Your cancellation can mean the opportunity for another client to spend time with your therapist. Cancelling is simple, common courtesy. Policies regarding the charge for cancelled appointments vary from one therapist to another. Understanding your therapist's billing procedures eliminates any surprises when you receive your statement.

When the Bill Comes Due

When you pay for your therapy will be up to your therapist. Many are more comfortable if you write a check for each session. They prefer that you do this prior to your appointment, rather than running overtime into their next session. Some therapists will bill you once a month, but will insist that you stay current on a monthly basis. You may run the risk of your therapy being terminated if you consistently fail to meet this agreement. However, in the event of an emergency such as a job loss, most allow you to make a special financial arrangement to continue your treatment and defer your payments for a short time.

If you know fairly early in your treatment that you will wish to see a therapist for, say, a year and you cannot afford his fee but you have some tangible assets, you may wish to borrow the money through a bank or other lending institution. Such requests can be listed "for medical care" on a loan application, which will eliminate having to discuss the details of your therapy needs with your banker.

Therapists in sole private practice are not always equipped for the paperwork involved in the use of credit cards, but some medical clinics, with an office staff, now accept major credit cards as a means of paying for therapy.

When You Don't Know Where to Go,
and You Have No Money

If you feel you need help and you are unable to afford a therapist's fee, one of the best ways to locate that help is by telephoning your County Mental Health Association. If you cannot locate the number in your telephone directory, your information operator can provide it to you.

When you telephone this association, one of the first question asked will be for your address. You will then be referred to the county mental health clinic nearest you, for an evaluation. In Los Angeles County, for example, there are thirty clinics at the present time. If you are in the midst of a crisis of any kind, for which mental health treatment is appropriate, a crisis evaluation treatment unit will begin helping you at once.

You are eligible for the services of a county mental health clinic if you are receiving welfare payments or Social Security benefits. You are also eligible if you have no funds at all or are unemployed. You will be screened to determine your present financial status, but no one is turned away because they lack funds.

Due to limited physical space, the treatment actually administered at mental health clinics is usually reserved for problems such as schizophrenia, manic depression, and other chronic mental illnesses, or for the trauma accompanying spousal abuse, battering, or rape.

But mental health clinics also act as a referral service for ongoing domestic problems and emotional difficulties requiring a less immediate response. In Los Angeles County, these referral locations include such state agencies as Family Services, where qualified applicants may receive assistance which includes counseling. Los Angeles County mental health clinics also refer applicants to the National Association of Social Workers, the California Graduate Counseling Center, and to teaching universities, all of whom charge a $20.00 initial fee and then a sliding scale fee of $5.00 to $15.00 per therapy appointment.

The County Mental Health Association in your area will have a similar list of referral sources for you to contact. These resources are helpful but there is usually a waiting list for the services, due to over-stressed county funding and frequent budget cutbacks.

If English is your second language, you may be referred to a therapist who speaks your preferred language. Or, you may be provided with an interpreter who can speak for you, if necessary, for short-term counseling. But this will not be a workable solution for long-term therapy, since the process of interpretation would intrude on the actual therapy work.

INSURANCE

If you have health insurance, call your insurance company or their local representative before your initial visit to find out whether your therapy is going to be covered. Ask about deductibles, required waiting periods for pre-existing conditions, and claim form submissions. Know what is in your insurance policy; it's part of being an informed consumer. And don't expect your therapist to act as an insurance expert. That's not included in the services for which you are paying.

Blue Cross, for example, will usually pay up to twenty percent (20%) of each therapy appointment, with an annual limit to the number of reimbursable visits, if you are seeing a licensed therapist. You will be paid from the beginning of your treatment, if you have no history of a pre-existing condition for the diagnosis given by your therapist. If you have a history of either this condition or of any diagnosed mental illness, you may have a waiting period of six months to one year before you are reimbursed. Most other insurance policies which cover therapy will have similar limitations.

5

Therapy Sessions
How They Work

• Your first appointment • What you provide • What your therapist provides • Why it works: trust, other essentials, and considerate therapy manners • Medications

YOUR FIRST APPOINTMENT

You don't have to pull yourself together for your first therapy appointment. Just go as you are, whether that's depressed, anxious, confused, angry, tearful, uncertain, or feeling nothing at all. Believe me, the therapist has seen it before. And an important part of you wants to be there *as you are*, or you would not have made the appointment.

The first session can be a little awkward for your new therapist, too. Why wouldn't it be? You're strangers. The fact that the therapist sees new people on a regular basis does not mean that the process is completely comfortable. You'll both get through it, and you won't be judged or criticized in any way.

Don't be disappointed if the first session isn't very exciting. Maybe it will be, but often the preliminary questions your therapist has to ask you can seem routine. However, a thorough documenting of your history is vital if you are to be helped. Your therapist must learn more about what your problems are, how your life is going, and what you are feeling.

If you underwent a mental health evaluation of the type described in Chapter Three, your therapist will weave the evaluation results together with the history notes from your first appointment, to form a psychological portrait of who you are when you meet. This brings your therapist up to date so you can begin to move forward together in dealing with your current issues.

When you get home from your first appointment, write down your impressions of the initial session in your Recovery Notebook. Include anything you felt especially positive about, and anything you felt apprehensive about. Allow yourself to explore your *initial* impressions of everything about that first session; your first impressions often reflect your deepest feelings. In addition, they may be a clue, for both of you, as to what underlying problems were "mirrored" by your therapist, and his surroundings, in this first meeting. This mirroring just means what you saw, heard, and felt, reflected an important part of you, that you'll deal with together. This writing will be used in your Six-Month Checkup with your therapist.

WHAT YOU PROVIDE TO YOUR THERAPIST

Your therapy session is not a weekly performance in which you have to impress your therapist with something memorable. Bringing yourself to your appointment is sufficient.

Usually, in the beginning, you and your therapist will be on a "get acquainted" mission. Although techniques vary among therapists, one way you'll work with your therapist is to describe, in your own words, what you did and how you felt during the week. Many clients use the Observations and Dreams sections of their Recovery Notebook to record this information. It can include items such as the following:

- who you spent time with and the nature of your activities;
- how you felt at work; at home; and with your family and friends;
- any time or situation when you were especially uncomfortable;
- any recurring thoughts that bothered you;
- any unusual behavior, something you did that you don't usually do; and,
- any dreams you can remember.

What you discuss with your therapist is certainly not limited to the issues just described. You will have plenty to talk about, from week to week, that is unique to you and your situation. And if you don't seem to have anything to say, your therapist will help you along and make it easy for you to discuss your feelings and problems.

WHAT YOUR THERAPIST PROVIDES

Your therapist will listen carefully to what you say about your thoughts, feelings, and actions during the week. Years of training and experience enable your therapist to trace the origin of your feelings and present possible reasons for any anxiety or depression you have. A therapist will help to interpret what your thoughts and dreams are trying to tell you about yourself, and suggest alternative ways to deal with other people. And whatever else is provided in therapy, you may be assured that your therapist will be there next week to help you, no matter what you say or how much pain you are in. Your therapist won't grow tired of you or your problems.

HOW THE PROCESS DEVELOPS

Together, you and your therapist establish a relationship based upon trust. Now you have a person with whom you are free to speak openly about all the issues in your life, and you have that person's undivided attention. For this reason, you may soon feel a sense of relief because you have begun to do something about your problems: you have found a good listener with whom to share them.

You develop more trust in your therapist from week to week, so you reveal yourself at increasingly deeper levels. And the more you reveal, the more insight and under-standing your therapist brings to your life and to your issues. As a result of this exchange, you begin to feel better and to respond with more interest and responsibility to the world around you. You also trust yourself and your own judgment at a deeper level. And you notice that you are more relaxed and trusting around other people.

Realistically, there are bumps in the road. But, once you're in therapy, at least you're on the road. There may be times you will want to quit but, if you maintain your commitment to be helped, this frustration passes and you recover in spite of it. Therapy is worth some occasional discomfort because it works so well most of the time.

THE ESSENTIALS

Don't expect a therapist to read your mind. Your therapist is well-trained to interpret what you say, to help you solve your problems. But a therapist is not able to "read" your thoughts and magically interpret your needs. A certain amount of "speaking up" will be required, and your therapist will help you learn to express what you need, as you work together.

Talk about everything that is giving you trouble, even when you would rather not admit it to yourself, or even if you think it's unimportant. Let your therapist decide, with you, what material is helpful to you.

Periodically, ask what you could be doing to help your therapy along. And share any writing you have done, including the exercises suggested in this book.

Don't expect your therapist to become your friend or to share a social life with you. Because your therapist wants to be as effective as possible in treating you, any other kind of relationship with you would not be desirable or useful to you.

CONFIDENTIALITY AND INFORMED CONSENT

In therapy, you have the same rights to client confidentiality that you have with your medical doctor. A therapist who violates that rule of confidentiality should be reported to your State Board of Medical Quality Assurance, and should be fired by you.

If your therapist suggests that any kind of mental health testing be administered to you, your informed consent must be obtained. You have a responsibility to yourself to understand the purpose of the testing, what the test results will be used for, and who will see the results. If anything about the testing procedure makes you uncomfortable, discuss it with your therapist.

TAKING MEDICATION

If you are taking any medication when you begin therapy, including medication for high blood pressure or low blood pressure, symptoms of menopause, anxiety, depression, or sleep disorders, be sure to inform your new therapist. These medications are known to cause changes in your consciousness, your emotional state, your thinking, your memory, your concentration, and your judgment—so of course they will affect your therapy process.

If your therapist recommends medication for you, find out when and how you are to take it, what the medication is intended to accomplish, and what side effects you may expect. Remember that only a medical doctor can prescribe medication so, unless your therapist is a psychiatrist, you will need a referral to a doctor for a medication evaluation and/or a prescription. If the idea of taking an antidepressant or antianxiety medication upsets you, by all means say so. Your therapist is not a mind reader, and your reassurance about medication is essential to your well being. If you won't take the medication, it can't help you.

Psychotropic medications (drugs which affect mental activity) do not solve your problems, or take the place of having to feel your emotions, or become a substitute for your therapy. They enable you to proceed with therapy and to cope with life while you and your therapist work together. And your dosage should never be reduced, increased, or discontinued by anyone but your therapist.

CONSIDERATE THERAPY MANNERS

If you are a smoker, ask your therapist's permission before you smoke anywhere in the office. You are on your therapist's turf and common courtesy is appropriate. Don't open up a three-course meal in the office, even if you *are* on your lunch hour. Arrange your meals to occur outside of therapy. And don't expect your therapist to return your phone calls on your timetable. Most therapists are on a fixed appointment schedule with little time between clients. If you have a genuine reason to phone your therapist, by all means do so. However, you should not make this a habit. Early in your therapy, you and your therapist should discuss any occasions when it would be necessary or appropriate for you to telephone.

The therapist's waiting room is not the place for children and friends to gather. Make baby-sitting arrangements in advance, and meet companions elsewhere, since this is usually a much smaller waiting room than the one in your doctor's office.

6

Tools
to Use on Your Own

• How your observations help your therapist • Why reporting your dreams is useful • How to get rid of secrets and resentments • How to survive your therapist's vacation • A relaxation technique • The Six-Month Checkup

YOUR OBSERVATIONS

Your view of the world is one of the most important tools in your therapy. As you grow and change, so do your impressions of everything in your life. You have arranged a section in your Recovery Notebook, entitled Observations, for recording notes about your week's activities and your feelings, plus any ideas you may have about your treatment. When read to your therapist, these notes help you both learn what was significant to you during the week. And they give your therapist insight about you that is not otherwise observable, because your therapist sees you only in a peaceful and consistent setting, minus the tensions of daily living.

As noted earlier, your observations will include how you felt at home, at work, and in your daily life. You should write down anything about your relationships that you think might be important, and unusual events that are not part of your normal routine. Also include any progress you noticed, on issues that you and your therapist have been discussing.

It isn't necessary to make a full time job of jotting down these observations. Writing in your Recovery Notebook is not intended to replace your life, or to help you avoid living it. A few minutes, several times a week, is probably sufficient for most clients. Here's a sample Observation page from Eileen's Recovery Notebook:

Remember to tell Dr. B. that, when I am frustrated, I get anxious. At work, Mr. H.'s smoking is driving me nuts. Have to do something, but what? I don't want to hurt his feelings and I don't want to breathe his smoke. Spent more money this week than I wanted to, but I think it's because J. hasn't called me and he said he would. Should I call him? Not yet, discuss first. Feel really good because I got a B+ in my history class.

Using the Observations section of your Recovery Notebook as Eileen has, to hit the highlights, often saves you time in therapy, and clarifies those areas that need attention in your session.

But there's another real bonus in writing down these observations regularly. The therapists interviewed for this book indicated that, when you observe yourself regularly, you are less likely to deceive yourself about anything, and self-deception creates both anxiety and depression. And the clients I interviewed who regularly use this "checking in" process noted a lessening of anxiety and depression, as well as enhanced self-confidence and trust in their own judgment. Once that trust in yourself is stabilized, you can begin to see how you may not need therapy forever!

Your Night Life - Dream On, but Write it Down

Dreams are important tools for therapy because your therapist works with your mind; when you go to sleep, your mind does not stop, but simply switches to another channel. Dreams are not random occurrences, as they might appear, but meaningful accounts of some part of the dreamer's life. This means your mind sends you and your therapist vital information in a different format than when you are awake.

But your dreams appear to you in symbols. The key appears to lie in breaking the code, for which you need an interpreter. That interpreter is your therapist. Freud felt that dreams contained both a hidden wish of the dreamer, like a "sleeping fantasy," and a defense against that wish, like a protective message warning you not to take on something dangerous. So dreams often present you with thoughts and feelings you cannot confront while you're awake; and they may also be trying to steer you onto a safe course of action in your waking life.

Another reason dreams can be valuable tools in your therapy is that they weave current experience and past experience together, almost like a rather jumbled mini-series. The real-life time sequence is often out of order but, when you and your therapist analyze them, helpful material is still available from your dreams, about both the past and the present.

You won't know how useful your dreams are unless you write them down and take them to therapy. Keep your Recovery Notebook on your nightstand, since dreams disappear from your consciousness about fifteen minutes after waking. It is not necessary to agonize over the content of a dream you can't remember. It will come back to you, in another dream, until the issue it represents is resolved for you, in therapy.

SECRETS

Don't keep secrets from your therapist. It just slows you down. Everything you talk about enables your therapist to make interpretations and give you helpful feedback. According to each of the therapists interviewed for this book, keeping secrets is also a common source of anxiety, much like the self-deception mentioned earlier. The more pressure there is on you, to keep the secret hidden, the more anxious you will feel.

If you become uncomfortable because you know you are withholding something from your therapist, it may help you to write about it in your Recovery Notebook, and then read this writing to your therapist. Molly has shared part of her writing with us:

I've been keeping this secret from my therapist, but I'm willing to at least write it down so I can look at it. The secret is that I'm afraid, really afraid, of being in small, closed spaces. It wasn't so bad before I came into therapy. In fact, it wasn't even the reason I started. So I don't really see the point of all this fuss about it, except that I keep thinking of it right before my sessions, and then I block it out.

Okay, now that I've written it down, what is the worst thing I can think of, that would happen if I told this to my therapist? Would he send me away and refuse to treat me? What do I have to gain by not telling my therapist this particular secret? Is there some payoff I don't want to give up?

Molly truly believed that, if she revealed her secret to her therapist, he would discontinue her treatment. She had been told by a friend that *claustrophobia* (fear of being in small spaces) was impossible to cure. Her friend was wrong, of course. Molly says her therapist didn't scold her; he didn't terminate her therapy; he didn't judge her; and he wasn't surprised. She concluded, "I know they can't read minds, but I think they have hunches, sometimes."

When you reveal your innermost secrets, don't be surprised if your therapist doesn't seem surprised. Most therapists have heard it all from other clients, and they are well-equipped to hear your secrets and then guide you through the next phase of your development.

RESENTMENTS

A resentment is some kind of anger you haven't been able to release. If you cling to it long enough, you can't concentrate on anything else. What began as an occasional irritation can become a life's work. Just as secrets may make you anxious, therapists agree that resentments, if not discussed and eventually discarded, may tend to make you feel depressed. Resentments are emotionally draining because they require a great deal of maintenance. Clinging to them can interfere with your work, your marriage, your social life and, most of all, your peace of mind.

In the course of your therapy you will eventually understand where your resentments come from and give them up; it's too uncomfortable to stay deeply resentful and move through your other issues at the same time. Here is how Rose dealt with her resentment toward a friend:

> *Sylvia and I have been friends for 25 years. She's generous with her time, and able to be there for me if I need help or a favor. So I had put off confronting the one thing Sylvia does that bothers me, because it just didn't seem important enough. What it is, is that Sylvia frequently invites other friends to join us when we have plans, without asking me first. I know how much she enjoys having people around and you'd think, after 25 years, it wouldn't upset me so much but it does.*

When Rose spoke with me, she said she had been placing other issues ahead of this resentment, in her therapy, so she wouldn't have to confront Sylvia. I suggested she write a letter to Sylvia and read it to her therapist. She never mailed it to Sylvia, of course.

In her session, Rose and her therapist discussed her resentment for Sylvia and the best way to deal with it. First, her therapist encouraged Rose to let go of her guilt and ambivalence for having these feelings for Sylvia. Then her therapist pointed out to Rose that she did not need to let Sylvia off the hook because of the length of their friendship, or because Sylvia was an otherwise desirable friend. He also indicated that Rose did not have to make a marathon event of confronting Sylvia. A few simple words, the next time the situation arose, would be sufficient. But Rose was only able to arrive at these understandings after first venting her feelings on paper, and then discussing the writing with her therapist.

If, as in Rose's case, you need assistance from your therapist in handling the situation involved in a resentment, it will help to have the thrust of your resentment in front of you, in black and white. Once you have ventilated your feelings, you and your therapist will be able to plan the appropriate action, if any is indicated. Here's the bare bones of such a letter:

Dear _____

I am really angry with you. I have felt this anger for a long time (or a short time) now, but I have not been able to express it to you directly. Carrying this anger is not good for me. I want to get rid of it. So here it is. . . .

The rest of the letter is up to you. Sometimes old resentments are entwined with positive, loving feelings for others, including family and friends, and your therapist will play a vital role in helping you to sort out this "mixed bag." But that is possible only if you bring the resentment to therapy, so you are encouraged to complete the letter above and take it to your session.

If the Resentment is for Your Therapist

Like it or not, what you have in therapy is two people who, periodically, may disagree. In fact, it would be surprising if they never did. If you develop a resentment for your therapist, and you have difficulty discussing it openly, you have three options. You can run to another therapist, and stay until you develop a resentment for that person, too. Secondly, you can use the sample writing exercise just described, and read the writing to your therapist.

If you go with option number two, you have the opportunity to disagree with a significant person in your life, and then observe yourself surviving the experience. It may seem harder and more uncomfortable than disagreeing with anyone else, but it's still better to discuss it with that significant person.

The third choice you have is keeping still about your complaint, which will eventually lead you out the door for good. Then your therapist won't ever know what happened, and you won't have a chance to grow. Donna shared the following experience with us:

Okay, I admit it, I did have a beef with my therapist. Group therapy was supposed to begin at 6:15, but people straggled in late and he waited till about 6:30 to start, and then he let the group run over, 15 minutes. I thought he knew I had to get home, but I guess I had miscommunicated and not told him. It was making me late to take my baby-sitter home, and I was getting so angry I was ready to leave the group. But I remembered your writing exercise, from your workshop and, instead of running away, I wrote the Resentment Letter to him.

I read the letter to my therapist in my individual session and he agreed with me and usually started the group on time after that. I don't think he liked me calling him on it, and I haven't been comfortable in group ever since. But if I had left before I did the writing, and not discussed it with Dr. D_____, I would never have known that I can stand up for myself with him. Now that I do know that, I have a skill I didn't have when I went in there. I guess if I get uncomfortable enough, I can always talk about it some more, too.

Donna learned a valuable lesson: when you have a resentment for your therapist, and you discuss it, your therapist will try to understand your point of view but may not react as you expect. Therapists are human too. Raising the resentment will still strengthen you, though. And growing stronger emotionally is one reason you are there.

SURVIVING YOUR THERAPIST'S VACATION

Eventually your therapist goes on vacation. In preparation for doing so, your therapist will have made arrangements with a colleague to take calls and to see clients, if necessary. But even if you are new to therapy, you will be pleasantly surprised at how well you do until your therapist returns. Most of us are stronger and more capable than we think. The tips below may lessen your apprehension.

Vacation Survival Kit

• When your therapist goes on vacation, *try not to make major changes in your life*, or commit to irreversible decisions, unless you have discussed them with your therapist in advance.

• If you encounter a problem, or you must make a decision, *ask yourself what your therapist would recommend*, if he or she were with you, and then do the best you can. You'll be surprised at how much you have already learned.

• And *take a little vacation of your own*. At the time you would usually be in your therapist's office, do something else you enjoy.

Your therapist will be able to add to these tips for making vacation times easier on you. Because of knowing you so well, your therapist will know just what recommendations to leave with you for that absence.

Calming Down

Learning to calm down and feel prepared to meet life's demands is always useful. This is vital to clients in therapy because, often, therapy clients are simultaneously experiencing daily, routine activities and inner, emotional changes. There are many elaborate and ritualized forms of meditation including Eastern, Western, formal, informal, and guided. But there is also a simple, calming way to contemplate your surroundings that can be as invigorating and restful as more complex forms of deep meditation.

Children use this refreshing resource every day; when we see them, we smile and acknowledge that they are "daydreaming again." But children have enormous resilience and energy that is partly obtained from the natural contemplation of their surroundings, which they enjoy so much.

This simple exercise requires no prescription or medical supervision. It can be done at home indoors, or out-of-doors, in a quiet, peaceful setting. First, place your body in a comfortable sitting position. With your eyes open, select an object of nature that is especially attractive to you, and begin to contemplate it. You might choose a favorite flower, plant or tree; a cloud formation; or a lake, lagoon, or nearby stream. Just relax and continue to focus comfortably on this object of nature.

Now, select one particular detail of your nature object and, without straining, contemplate that detail. This might be a specific leaf formation; the petals of just one rose; the lacy edges of one cloud above you; or a ripple in a lagoon or stream. Observe the changes, the movement, and the continuum of just that detail of your nature object.

When practiced daily, for about 15 minutes, this exercise can be beneficial in reducing tension by shifting your attention away from your obsessive thoughts, your problems, your unmet needs, and anything else with which you are struggling. Contemplation is not intended to solve anything, and there is no incorrect way to do it. Just relax your body and pick a nature object. This simple exercise was reportedly employed by the late President John F. Kennedy, who referred to it as the emotional equivalent of a catnap.

It is also helpful to enter your therapy appointments in a quiet, peaceful state of being, if possible. If you can arrive a few minutes early, this time can be used beneficially by simply closing your eyes and breathing deeply, to relax. You will feel under less pressure when you begin your session and you will be amazed at how much tension ebbs away in five minutes of doing absolutely nothing.

THE SIX-MONTH CHECKUP

When you've been in therapy for about six months, refer to your Therapy Notebook for the original issues that brought you into therapy, your life goals, your first impressions of your therapist, and your wildest fantasies. Your observations and feelings about this partnership are important to you and to your therapist. You both want to know if it is really working for you, and six months is enough time to answer the questions below.

In a quiet, undistracted setting, write down whatever comes into your mind in response to the questions below. Do not edit your first responses to these questions, because they will probably reflect your truest beliefs about your therapy experience so far. The next time you go to therapy, spend some time in your session dealing with this Six-Month Checkup. You're on a path in therapy and this checklist is part of your road map.

Part One - The Partnership

1. Do you feel comfortable with your therapist at this time?

2. Do you find it easy to confide in your therapist?

3. How accurate were your first impressions of your therapist?

4. Were you apprehensive about anything after your first session?

5. Has that concern gone away, improved, or stayed the same?

6. Have you shared that concern with your therapist?

7. Do you feel you have any unfinished business with your therapist?

8. If so, what is the nature of this business?

By now, you will have some idea of what you really think of this therapist, including whether or not you trust your therapist, how you feel about the process, and whether you look forward to your sessions. If you are not one hundred percent comfortable with your therapist, you need to discuss anything that is bothering you.

Part Two - Goals

1. Do you sense progress with the living problems for which you hired a therapist?

2. Are you feeling more hopeful about your life than you did when you began therapy?

3. Are you more in touch with your feelings than when you began therapy?

4. Of the goals you had for yourself, before you began treatment, are any completed?

5. What is the status of your remaining goals?

6. What do you believe is involved in the completion of these goals?

The answers to these questions will give you some idea of what you have already accomplished. One reason it is important to complete this check list, and discuss it in therapy, is to see how much progress you have made in only six months. Most clients work hard in therapy from week to week, but they fail to reflect upon the fruits of their labor. It is important to do so, because we all need hope. Your Six-Month Checkup is designed, in part, to provide that hope.

Part Three - Fantasies

Earlier in this book, I suggested that you write down all your wildest fantasies before you began therapy. Your fantasies tell you and your therapist a great deal about you. Fantasy is the source of your ideas, inspirations, creativity, and imagination. And fantasy can be a clue to some experience you desire, or to the kind of person you aspire to become.

For all these reasons, it is helpful to your therapist to know *where* your mind goes when it wanders. These fantasies could include wanting to pursue more education or a promotion at work; owning a dream house you think you could never afford; improving the condition of your neighborhood, or of society; or just having more time to yourself.

Here's the Six-Month Checkup, as it is related to your fantasies:

1. How many of the fantasies on your list are still desirable to you, after this six months in therapy?

2. If you have discarded any of them, why have you done so?

3. As you now know yourself, how realistic are the fantasies still remaining on your list?

4. Will they be good for you or will they hurt you? Will they hurt anyone else?

5. Is there anything you can do to attain your fantasies that you are not doing?

6. Are you willing to commit, now, to the footwork of making your fantasies a reality?

7. If not, why?

8. Now that you know yourself better, are there any fantasies you'd like to *add* to your list, and work toward?

This Six-Month Checkup, when completed by you and discussed with your therapist, should give you a fair assessment of how you feel about therapy; your progress so far; where you have yet to travel; and what you may have to do to get there. You're not flying completely blind, because you have a guide and a map, but you also don't want to miss the side trips you can't anticipate. Side trips are encouraged in therapy. They are also inevitable and your therapist is expecting them. These side trips include sudden "overnight" insights about a problem you didn't think you were working on at all. Or an unexpected but welcome attitude of forgiveness or compassion you didn't know was missing within you. Or a big change is someone *else's* way of relating to you, that you didn't anticipate. It's a blessing that we can't chart the course of therapy so precisely that we miss these benefits.

After six months in therapy, it is hoped that you are looking forward to your sessions, that your therapist has become a trusted confidante, and that the work you do is helping you. If all this is not true, you need to consider why these reasonable expectations are unmet. Then you need an honest discussion about it, with your therapist. A therapist expects you to talk about any discouragement or disappointment you feel about your therapy. You can't be helped with it if you don't talk about it. This doesn't have to be an elaborate or intense conversation; but all partnerships require periodic, open assessment, and therapy is no exception.

You may also wish to use those particular questions that apply to you, for an annual "inventory" of your progress in therapy and to give direction to you and your therapist, as you continue to grow and to change. At those annual inventory times, you may wish to refer back to this first Six-Month Checkup, to note your progress.

Section Three

This section addresses four specific issues for which many people have found therapy useful. They were chosen for inclusion because of their prevalence in our culture today. They are:

1. Help for people from dysfunctional or alcoholic families who need Self Parenting skills and treatment for co-dependency.

2. The treatment of alcoholism and drug addiction, and the effectiveness of therapy in combination with Alcoholics Anonymous.

3. Eating disorders, including compulsive overeating, anorexia, and bulimia, and how therapy and Overeaters Anonymous work successfully together in their treatment.

4. How therapy and Debtors Anonymous create a combined solution for compulsive spending.

7

Therapy
for the Way You Grew Up

• *The purpose of childhood* • *The Inner Child and the Inner Parent* • *Self Parenting for people from dysfunctional families* • *What co-dependency is and how therapy can help*

HOW CHILDREN BECOME ADULTS

There is no perfect childhood. Preoccupied, well-meaning human beings are called upon to raise needy, defenseless children. But, much of the time, human resilience persists; the effort is rewarding and joyful; and children are transformed into functional adults. They learn *how* to become adults by watching their parents and others in their environment. This is an essential function of childhood. Ideally, children are also encouraged to play, and to enjoy being alive, which is vital to their well-being.

In a home that fulfills children's essential needs, children develop more or less unconsciously, without having to *think* about what comes next. They feel increasingly prepared for life, into adolescence and young adulthood. They learn what their biologic, social, emotional, and intellectual needs are and, most of the time, they know how to meet those needs. These children can also enlist alternative resources when they feel stuck. They enter into early adult life with little or no damage from childhood.

But in a family where the first priority is alcohol or drugs, compulsive spending, or overeating, for example, children's developmental needs are not well met. Often they are left to their own devices prematurely, so they *must* think about what comes next, to the point of preoccupation. Sadly, they are also apt to be victims of physical, verbal, or sexual abuse. These same children often become drug abusers, alcoholics, compulsive spenders, or overeaters themselves. Many develop learning disabilities and disciplinary problems as well.

Adults from dysfunctional families report sensing a lifelong emotional distance between themselves and their parents. Therapists observe that many of them still yearn to achieve a late, close bond with their parents, into midlife. They are often either resentful workaholics or they are unable to retain a job at all, attempting to transfer the responsibility for their unmet emotional needs to their "work family."

As adults, people from addictive families may also have sexual difficulties or lack appropriate information about sex. Many feel unprepared for dating, marriage, and parenthood because they feel vaguely unfinished with their own childhoods. Their friendships often fail due to their unrealistic expectations of others. Additionally, they make grandiose promises to themselves which they are rarely able to keep. Much of the time, they report feeling either angry or depressed about life, themselves, and their future.

If you identify with the characteristics noted above, the situation isn't hopeless. You will need a return trip home to assess the extent of the damage. You don't really go home to do this, of course. You do it in therapy, and Self Parenting can help. With your therapist, you will repair that damaged toddler's emotional system, acquire the living skills you missed as an adolescent, and launch a more informed re-entry into adulthood. This is all accomplished by taking one small step at a time, at your own pace, and with no pressure to attempt more than you can accomplish. You will begin by attending to the child you used to be.

Inner Child, Inner Parent, and Self Parenting

Your Inner Child is your own voice from childhood. Your Inner Parent is the combined internalized voice of both your parents, as you perceive them, also from your childhood. If you are from a dysfunctional family, both the Inner Child and the Inner Parent parts of your personality are missing important information we all need, in order to cope with life.

One successful method of repairing this damage from childhood is found in John Pollard's book, *Self Parenting*. To quote Pollard, "You, as the Inner Parent, must assume the role of loving, supporting, and nurturing your Inner Child. By doing so, you can make your life full and satisfying for the first time since you were a child, and keep it that way for the rest of your life." (P.142).

In Chapter One of this book, your Inner Child was given a special section in your Recovery Notebook. In that section, you may now wish to respond to the questions below. Your Inner Child is encouraged to answer the questions as simply or as completely as desired. Your Inner Parent is urged not to judge or criticize your Inner Child's responses, because there are no right or wrong answers to these questions. Although it may feel somewhat awkward, thinking from two different parts of yourself for a few minutes will help you learn things about yourself that you may have forgotten.

- Inner Child, how are you feeling right now?

- Inner Child, how did you sleep last night?

- Inner Child, can you tell me about a time when you were sad?

- Inner Child, what do you like to do for fun?

Pollard's book contains a starter kit of such questions, which initiate a direct dialogue with the child you once were.

How Therapy Can Help with Self Parenting

Phil, who is from a dysfunctional family, had been in individual therapy once a week and had also been doing daily Self Parenting exercises for about a year-and-a-half.

I asked him to tell us how he felt before he entered treatment for his issues from childhood:

Well, I often felt lonely in the presence of others. But on the other hand, I often felt crowded and suffocated on the inside, even when I was alone! I guess I never learned to share deep feelings with another person. I felt almost childish at work. Some years, my marriage was empty and unsatisfying, and other years it was a battleground with no winners. I didn't feel prepared to be a parent myself. I had this sense that my major life decisions never had my own support. I never did trust life, or myself, and I used to change my mind about fifty times a day, about everything. I never seemed to have enough energy. Oh, and I was anxious. Other than that, things were okay.

At first, Phil resisted his therapist's suggestion that changing his mind frequently was at all related to his anxiety. He noted:

I felt robbed of my spontaneity. But in the course of my Self Parenting writing exercises, I learned I had never listened to that kid inside, who gets scared when I say one thing and do another! First, the poor kid couldn't trust my parents, and then he couldn't trust me. I can see how I'd be anxious.

Phil read his Self Parenting writing to his therapist on a regular basis. As his therapist heard the thoughts, feelings, and beliefs of Phil's Inner Child, they were able, together, to identify the specific childhood issues with which Phil needed help. Since Phil had no model for this guidance, as a child, it was necessary for him to "build" an Inner Parent. After several months of Self Parenting exercises and therapy, Phil's anxiety lessened, and he gradually became more productive and fulfilled.

The changes you make in therapy will affect not only you, but also the significant people in your life. Phil now feels less dependent upon his wife, and the quality of their relationship has improved. But, early in Phil's recovery from his dysfunctional family, this couple required marital counseling when his wife expressed fears that Phil would become less dependent upon her and leave her. She was used to meeting his needs at the expense of her own, which frequently caused her to pick fights with Phil when she felt deprived or unappreciated. She has recently begun to do the Self Parenting exercises for herself each morning.

For Phil, and for others who can benefit from the experience of learning to Self Parent, a therapist with the qualities outlined in previous chapters is essential. But this therapy will also require a therapist with specific training and experience in working with the Inner Child. This therapist can help you initiate and maintain a consistent dialogue with your Inner Child, and can also teach you how to meet your current needs in appropriate adult ways. In time, you will be able to turn off the radio station in your head that is tuned to your critical Inner Parent from childhood. Your Inner Child will eventually learn to trust the wise guidance being received from the new Inner Parent.

If this material seems helpful to you, refer to Pollard's book, listed at the end of this book, under Recommended Readings. And when you are interviewing potential therapists, inquire about their work with the Inner Child and the Inner Parent.

CO-DEPENDENCY DEFINED AND TREATED

Everyone enjoys, to some extent, the satisfaction of helping another. But if you feel that you must regularly rescue another person, or meet their needs at the expense of your own, you are co-dependent.

If you came from an alcoholic, addictive, or dysfunctional family, the chances are great that your therapy will require some attention to co-dependency. According to Robert Ackerman and Susan Pickering, coauthors of *Abused No More*: "Negative ways of thinking and behaving that result from living with someone who is addicted to alcohol or other drugs is known as co-dependency." (P.15).

Co-dependency is a belief. If you are co-dependent, you believe that another person will be able to make you feel complete.

Co-dependency is a feeling. If you are co-dependent, you feel an urgent need to be close to that other person, at all costs.

Co-dependency is a way of behaving. If you are co-dependent, you will alternately try to please and manipulate that other person and, often, put up with some form of abuse from that person.

Ackerman and Pickering also say that, "In the alcoholism field, the last decade has seen a growing recognition of co-dependency as a condition affecting all members of the addictive family." (P.15). To their compelling statement, I would add, affecting *especially* the children.

Many of these children learned less than effective ways of relating to other people. As adults, their arguments in defense of their co-dependency often include:

- *But we are taught to help others.*
- *What about the Golden Rule?*
- *We are, in a sense, our brother's keeper.*
- *We're all in the same boat.*
- *There's nothing wrong with wanting to make my loved ones happy.*

Right on every count. But if you are co-dependent, your problem is threefold: the *degree* to which you are driven to carry out this excessive care-taking; the *powerlessness* you feel over your co-dependent behavior; and your inability to feel any genuine *self-esteem* when you are acting out co-dependent behavior.

Co-dependent people often report feeling unable to stop themselves from behaving in this manner, as if they are powerless to govern their own thinking and relating, regarding the other individual. This is partly because the origin of co-dependency is usually deeply rooted in childhood, during a time of life when we are all powerless, to a great extent, over the actions and behavior of our parents. Co-dependent behavior is, in fact, so thoroughly ingrained that a reliable sense of one's self, and what it means to be you, as separate from others, is missing or badly damaged in co-dependent people. This makes it impossible to experience any self-esteem or to value one's own separate existence or achievements.

Regarding positive feelings, many co-dependents reported, when interviewed for this book, that they felt they only "belonged" or "felt joyful" when their behavior was appreciated and complimented by another person. They related being unable to feel good about being who they are, as an ongoing function of their own personalities and their daily living.

Two of the driving forces behind co-dependent behavior are a deep-seated fear of abandonment, and an obsessive desire to please others. Let's see how these stressors affected two clients in treatment for co-dependency.

Fear of Abandonment

Lana is a co-dependent. She had trouble maintaining nurturing intimate relationships with men, which dated from her damaged alliance with her father. She was never sure where she left off, emotionally, and the man began, or what "rights" she had in a relationship. Lana felt her behavior going out of control when she began to follow her boyfriend each time he left his home. Although she entered therapy in order not to lose her boyfriend, Lana had actually taken the first step in her recovery from co-dependency.

Her therapy involved the thorough examination of her relationships with her father, other relatives, the men she dated, the people with whom she worked, and all of her social acquaintances. Lana was encouraged to be rigorously honest with her therapist about what she was *really* doing and saying with these other people, and what she was feeling, as she took the painful steps toward establishing firm ways of stating her needs and desires to others.

This honesty enabled her therapist to assist Lana in developing the relating skills necessary which had been missing in her family of origin. Her therapist also pointed out to Lana that her emotional insecurity had a foundation in reality. Lana's mother had so displeased her father, by returning to work when Lana was born, that he left them. His abandonment was compounded by the absence of a mother who needed to work. So Lana grew up believing that she must avoid the repetition of that abandonment at all costs.

The change in Lana's feelings when she began, tremulously, to put her *own* needs first, was exciting to her. As she put it:

> *I felt comforted in the knowledge that I could meet my own needs; that it was not anyone else's job anyway; and that no one I know is going to perish if I can't meet their expectations. As long as I don't abandon myself, I can do pretty well, now.*

Dying to Please

Like Lana, Danny is a co-dependent. He was the oldest of five children who became the man of the house when his alcoholic father left the family in Danny's teens. No matter how much help he contributed to his family, Danny never felt it was enough.

Early in his career as a hospital maintenance worker, Danny's co-dependency revealed itself in two significant ways: he felt he had to accomplish more than his co-workers, just to keep his job, so he often worked later than other employees. He also frequently said "Yes" to requests made by his supervisor, when saying "No" would have been more appropriate. As Danny told his therapist:

> *I felt compelled to stay late at work, like someone was pulling my strings, like I wasn't in charge of my life at all. Almost possessed.*

When Danny received a promotion, his drinking and partying with his buddies after work escalated into a problem that threatened his job. He sensed he wanted to sabotage his promotion but, on some level, he also wanted it.

At the insistence of his wife, Danny entered therapy. He was able to examine his apprehension about his new managerial role; to be honest with his therapist about his current alcohol intake; and to identify his lifelong fear that he would fail to be accepted by others.

In therapy Danny became more comfortable in his supervisory position. Together, he and his therapist also dealt with his long-standing fear of displeasing others. His therapist referred Danny to A.A. meetings to determine, for himself, whether he felt he was an alcoholic. As Danny explained to me:

> *When I went into therapy, I couldn't spell co-dependent. Now I am one, and I'm glad, because it's got a cure!*

In the early stages of co-dependency, you may be blissfully unaware of your co-dependent beliefs, feelings and behavior, as described earlier. You may even seek therapy for some other issue in the beginning. But planting you in the client chair in therapy means slowly developing self-awareness. Eventually, it becomes difficult to hide your co-dependency or leave it in the waiting room.

Once you see the problem, you may feel somewhat impatient to be rid of it. But, although co-dependency is certainly a candidate for treatment in therapy, it takes time. The solution will consist of finding out *why* you have been relating co-dependently to other people; working with your therapist to devise healthier ways of relating to others; and a lot of practice with the skills your therapist presents.

You can't change the past, but you can certainly overcome it. Therapy, combined with Self Parenting techniques, is frequently successful in repairing the damage of a less-than-adequate start in life. And the characteristics of co-dependency you inherited need not remain among your solutions. If your childhood is giving you problems today, there is therapy for the way you grew up.

CHAPTER

8

When Alcohol
is the Problem

*• How a family alcoholism intervention works • Inpatient
treatment for alcoholism • A look at Alcoholics Anonymous
and therapy for the alcoholic client.*

Alcoholism kills. The problem of alcoholism has reached
epidemic proportions in our culture. According to the
National Council on Alcoholism, the effects of alcoholism
cost our nation's employers nearly 90 billion dollars in
1987. The employee with alcohol problems, and the family
members of problem drinkers, experience a decline in
productivity and incur excessive absenteeism and tardiness.
In addition, many deny that the problem is their alcoholism and, instead, blame the workplace for their difficulties,
and then file costly and unnecessary Workers' Compensa-
tion lawsuits against their employers.

The Council noted, in addition, that approximately 25,000 deaths, or nearly one-half of all U.S. highway fatalities in 1987, and 600,000 traffic-related injuries, were caused by drivers abusing alcohol. Also in 1988, an estimated 67 percent of U.S. homicide offenders and 50 percent of reported rape cases were committed while the perpetrator was drinking.

The erosion of American family life, from alcoholism, is tragic. Robert Ackerman and Susan Pickering, authors of *Abused No More*, stated, "Although most alcoholics will tell you that their drinking does not affect anyone but them, there are approximately 40 million non-alcoholic spouses and children of alcoholics who will tell you otherwise . . . while waiting for their (the alcoholic's) sobriety, families fall apart, marriages collapse, abuse continues, and children grow up and leave home . . . there is no such thing as a non-abusive alcoholic relationship" (Pp. 65, 69, 87).

Our fantasies of the homeless, wine-abusing drunk, down on his luck, no longer serve us, for alcoholism ravages the lives and families of rich, middle class, and poor; white, black, brown, and red; teens to retirees. In this chapter, we will see how therapy is useful in treating alcoholism, in conjunction with Alcoholics Anonymous.

FAMILY INTERVENTION

If you saw the television version of Betty Ford's story, or you read about her triumph over alcoholism, you remember that her sobriety began with her husband and children confronting her with love and concern for her well-being. They recalled the times her drinking had led the family to despair and they offered support through her upcoming recovery, if she would submit to hospitalization.

This process is called a family intervention. In Mrs. Ford's case, it led her from a California detoxification center to the founding of the Betty Ford Center for the treatment of alcoholism and drug abuse.

For alcoholics or drug addicts who can no longer care for themselves, intervention has proven beneficial in providing feedback from family members, loved ones, and associates. However, until the alcoholic is ready to admit to problems that cannot be solved alone, he or she will probably continue to abuse alcohol or drugs and suffer the often fatal consequences. But, if an alcoholic is ready to recover, an intervention followed up by a well-functioning inpatient program can save the alcoholic's life.

How One Intervention Worked

David, age 44, had been abusing alcohol for several years. He had threatened his wife when drinking, on at least a dozen occasions. He had done considerable damage to their home while drinking. He had two major auto accidents in six months while driving in alcoholic blackouts. He had threatened their two teenage sons with physical abuse. And he had lost four sales positions in three years as a result of his drinking.

David's life was out of control. His abuse of alcohol was destroying his life and his family. When David had an alcoholic seizure at home his wife, Judy, called their family physician who suggested a family intervention to break through David's denial about the seriousness of his alcohol problem, and enable him to accept help.

After a tour of the chemical dependency unit, and an introduction to the staff, Judy and her children were encouraged to write down anything they would like to say to David about how his alcoholism had disrupted their lives. Then, without David present, his family members rehearsed with the alcoholism counselor for the upcoming confrontation in a safe and controlled atmosphere. Here were some of the messages that they wanted David to hear:

Chris, his older son: *Dad, I'm afraid to ride in the car with you anymore, when you've been drinking.*

Judy: *I'm afraid to leave you alone anymore. I'm scared to death your cigarette will burn the house down someday, when you're passed out on the sofa, drunk.*

Harvey, his younger son: *Dad, you can hide the vodka bottle when my friends come over, but we can still tell when you've been drinking, by your slurred speech and your staggering. It embarrasses me so much I just don't bring anybody around, now.*

Judy: *I still love you, David, but I can't count on you anymore for anything. I don't want to put up with your drinking and this intervention is the last way I have, to tell you I love you, but I'm scared for you.*

The alcoholism counselor urged David's family to keep their messages short, direct, and current. This initial meeting with David would not be a gripe session about the

second honeymoon that never came, or the ruined Thanks-
giving dinner five years ago. Those confrontations would
come later. At the moment, David's present, life-threaten-
ing behavior with alcohol was their first priority.

Any hesitation, guilt, or reluctance on the part of
David's family about confronting him with his problem was
also addressed in this meeting. The counselor encouraged
their sons, Chris and Harvey, to begin attending meetings
of Adult Children of Alcoholics, and he directed Judy to
meetings of Al-Anon, for spouses of alcoholics.

The next step was a formal confrontation between
David and his family in the presence of the hospital's alcoholism counselor. This gathering was met with considerable hostility and denial by David. The family was prepared for his resistance. They had been told that alcoholics,
when confronted, frequently feel conspired against by their
loved ones, especially if they are not ready to stop drinking.

David calmed down enough to listen to his family's
heartfelt messages of concern, but he expressed great fear,
since he had never tried to quit drinking before. It was
suggested that he attempt a trial period of sobriety with
the understanding that, if he failed, he would enter the
chemical dependency unit. David reluctantly agreed to try
to stay sober, and he got drunk on two occasions in the
next nine days.

During David's unsuccessful attempt to manage and
control his drinking, Judy began to attend meetings of Al-
Anon, and their two teenagers became active in the
Twelve-Step program of Adult Children of Alcoholics. As

a result, his family no longer made a fuss over David, or made excuses to friends for his being off work. They wisely pursued their own lives rather than be manipulated and ruled by David's alcoholism. David later said he had never felt so lonely and so ignored in the presence of his family as he had in those nine days:

> *They stepped around me or over me. They came and went as if I was invisible. I felt bereft. And the more I thought about my pain, the more I wanted to drink. It was a nightmare.*

As a result of his changed home environment, and his inability to stop drinking on his own, David admitted defeat and pursued hospitalization for his alcoholism. He now attends outpatient meetings of A.A. in the hospital where he became sober, and his family continues to attend support group meetings on a regular basis.

This family opted to remain together and work through the issues surrounding David's alcoholism. But, just as often, alcoholism rips a family apart at the seams. Sometimes these broken families can be repaired; sometimes they cannot. Still, regardless of the family situation, the alcoholic is always encouraged to strive for sobriety. If an alcoholic stops drinking to win back a spouse, children, or a job, the first criticism or difficulty the alcoholic encounters can produce a sufficient resentment to become drunk again in a matter of hours "to show them."

An intervention may appear to be a failure in the immediate sense, if the alcoholic continues to drink. But the seeds of sobriety have been planted. These honest, clear concerns, spoken by loved ones, can be enormously persuasive reasons for the alcoholic to stop drinking later on.

What Inpatient Treatment is Like

Inpatient treatment takes place in a specialized alcoholism or substance abuse unit which is either part of a psychiatric hospital, part of a general hospital, or a freestanding rehabilitation unit. Inpatient treatment allows the alcoholic a "running head start" at four to six weeks of sobriety in a structured environment. It is useful in treating alcoholics who require medical treatment for seizures or alcohol-related physical illnesses. But it is often possible for people to achieve sobriety without hospitalization, through attendance at Alcoholics Anonymous meetings, which are free to the alcoholic.

The support provided by the staff in inpatient treatment enables the alcoholic to learn that feelings of frustration can be directed into healthier forms of expression than the immediate gratification of alcohol. Here the alcoholic can begin to enjoy *not drinking*, and can then develop confidence in an alcohol-free lifestyle.

THE STAFF MEMBERS AND WHAT THEY DO

The Psychiatrist

This doctor will be able to determine what psychiatric or personality disorders are present in the recovering alcoholic. In addition, the psychiatrist can prescribe medication for the complications of withdrawal, such as seizures and delirium tremens. Often, a psychiatrist acts as the program director of a chemical dependency unit, and he is the leader of the treatment team.

The Psychologist

This team member is skilled in group therapy dynamics and also qualified as an individual therapist. The psychologist participates in the client's initial evaluation and treatment planning. He or she may perform psychological testing to determine whether the newly sober alcoholic has any neurologic problems, or is suffering from anxiety, which can be helped by therapy. Often, this team member conducts group and individual therapy sessions attended by the client during hospitalization, and is available to assist other members of the treatment team.

The Alcoholism Counselor

Trained staff members who are also recovering alcoholics are acutely sensitive to the alcoholic's denial system. What they say is sometimes more acceptable to clients because recovering alcoholism counselors are sharing their own past experiences with alcoholism. Alcoholism counselors often participate in the initial family intervention, if one is required. They provide the client with information on the Twelve Steps of Alcoholics Anonymous. They discuss the role of the client's long-repressed, emerging emotions in recovery. They also conduct group sessions with the client and the client's family on confronting defenses, viewing alcoholism as a disease, and developing continuing self-care tools.

Staff members who are not alcoholics, but who come from alcoholic families, are also useful in the role of alcoholism counselor, and their training must fulfill the same requirements. The experience of having grown up in an alcoholic home, or having been in an alcoholic marriage, may enable the staff member to be especially sensitive to the family's or spouse's needs while the client is confined to the hospital. But, as with the recovering alcoholic, their effectiveness as members of the helping profession depends upon receiving treatment for their own family alcoholism.

The Nurses

The nurses in an inpatient facility are among the first people you should cultivate if this chapter in any way impacts on your life. They are invaluable to relatives and loved ones because they spend a great deal of time with their clients. Often, their personal interest in the newly recovering alcoholic can contribute as much to recovery as the more formal therapy sessions.

The Social Workers

Alcoholism is a family disease affecting the spouse, the children, and the home environment of the alcoholic, as was demonstrated in David's story. The social worker in an inpatient alcoholism treatment facility usually focuses on the family of the client, once the client is hospitalized. The social worker will conduct an evaluation to determine whether other members of the family are dependent on alcohol or drugs; how that is affecting the designated client and what may be done about it; and whether the current make-up of the family system is enabling the alcoholic to remain ill.

From this data, the social worker designs a treatment plan for the family, which may include family therapy and attendance at Twelve-Step meetings. As the client recovers in the treatment facility, the social worker continues to monitor the family's progress.

ALCOHOLICS ANONYMOUS: A VITAL TOOL

Once the alcoholic is sober, deeply felt, underlying emotions come to attention suddenly and painfully. A vital ingredient to recovery at that point is Alcoholics Anonymous, a voluntary self-help organization offering assistance to persons who have a desire to stop drinking. No one in A.A. identifies anyone else as an alcoholic. You attend meetings and decide, for yourself, whether your drinking is a problem. There are no dues or fees for joining Alcoholics Anonymous.

What alcoholics find in A.A. meetings, that is vital to their emotional well-being, is hope for a better way of life. Much information about alcoholism is contained in the book *Alcoholics Anonymous*, written by recovering alcoholics themselves. If alcoholism affects you in any way, you are encouraged to read this book.

The Twelve Steps of A.A. are intended to convey to the alcoholic the importance of not drinking; of making amends for past behavior; of trusting in some kind of spiritual experience; and of helping other alcoholics to recover. In the initial step of A.A.'s Twelve Steps, the alcoholic is asked to concede that drinking has made life unmanageable. Once this admission is made, the alcoholic is felt to be on the road to recovery. The second step deals with alcoholic insanity, that repetitious behavior often engaged in by alcoholics in which, under the influence of alcohol, they find themselves hoping that the results of their drinking bouts will be different the next time. The newcomer to A.A. is asked only to believe that a power greater than the alcoholic can restore sound judgment to a mind warped with this self-destructive thinking. In the beginning of one's membership in A.A., this power may simply be the large numbers of recovering A.A. members everywhere, and especially those in his or her home group, who have found a better way to live. The third of A.A.'s twelve steps asks that the newcomer decide to surrender to the care of this power. It is often at this point that the newcomer selects a sponsor and begins to receive further guidance about living sober. More about sponsorship is explained below.

The fourth and fifth steps of Alcoholics Anonymous ask that the alcoholic write a thorough inventory of the damage done while drinking, and share that inventory with another person, usually the sponsor. A therapist or clergyman is also suggested as an alternative individual to hear one's inventory. After listening to this inventory, the sponsor often guides the new member into the sixth through ninth steps of the A.A. program. The sixth and seventh steps help the alcoholic become more familiar with those defects of character which caused alcoholic behavior in the first place, and how to deal with them in sobriety.

The eighth and ninth steps involve creating a list of those people the alcoholic harmed while drinking, and then making direct amends to those people. The tenth step enables the alcoholic to continue this process of prompt admission to wrongdoing, on a daily basis.

Regarding the spiritual aspects of this fellowship, Alcoholics Anonymous takes a nondenominational approach. This program is not affiliated with any church, religious sect, or specific definition of God. The newcomer is simply asked to begin cleaning up the wreckage of the past drinking life, and to believe that a spiritual awakening will follow, which will allow a comfortable and useful life without drinking. The nature of this spiritual experience is defined in the eleventh of A.A.'s twelve steps.

The twelfth step of A.A. urges alcoholics to rekindle the joy of living in the mainstream of life that most once knew, but to do so without alcohol. It also stresses the importance of the service aspect of the fellowship, noting that much personal fulfillment is to be gained by sponsoring other newcomers and by accepting various service commitments at A.A. meetings.

Sponsorship

The newly recovering alcoholic who attends A.A. meetings associates with people who no longer use alcohol to solve their living problems. In time, through this exposure, constructive solutions to problems replace the old, destructive ways of dealing with life.

The newcomer is encouraged to ask another member to become his or her A.A. sponsor, a person who provides guidance through the Twelve Steps. This guidance also involves the newcomer checking in with the sponsor, sometimes daily, to report activities and feelings about newfound sobriety. In a caring, nonjudgmental way, a sponsor can assist the recovering alcoholic in making living decisions while alcohol-free, and in understanding new feelings which the alcoholic had long denied.

In most A.A. groups, it is recommended that newly recovering women seek female sponsors, and that men work with men. Until some stability in sobriety is achieved, the issues of sexuality and dating usually only add more pressure to the newcomer's life.

It is essential for recovering alcoholics to resolve their living problems, to accept conditions as they are, and to be honest about their emotions, lest resentments build which can lead to the first drink. In A.A. meetings, alcoholics repeatedly hear the stories of other members who *thought* they could drink again and start recovery over again later—only to begin drinking and die. Although statistics are difficult to compile, many A.A. members of long standing agree that, in their experience, a second chance is far less likely than the alcoholic, curled up with a resentment and a bottle, thinks it is.

How A.A. Feels About the Use of Therapy

According to the book, *Alcoholics Anonymous*, "God has abundantly supplied this world with fine doctors, psychologists, and practitioners of various kinds. Do not hesitate to take your health problems to such persons. . . . We should never belittle a good doctor. . . . Their services are often indispensable in treating a newcomer. . . ." (P. 33).

How Therapy Helps the Recovering Alcoholic

While still drinking, an alcoholic may attend years of therapy and not change much. This is because the alcoholic's living problems are so deeply buried under the drinking problem that neither the alcoholic nor the therapist can locate them. The alcoholic withholds what is really going on, in order to protect and guard the abuse of alcohol.

Once sober, however, the alcoholic can benefit from treatment with a therapist who is knowledgeable about alcoholism. For one thing, the sober alcoholic has removed the first layer of distorted thinking just by putting down the bottle. After taking this major step, the alcoholic is able to explore, with the therapist, what needs to be repaired in life.

Perhaps, for example, the alcoholic has been unable to hold a job due to excessive drinking. Using the therapist as a temporary job counselor, among other roles, is helpful. No one will know the alcoholic's immediate financial needs and capabilities better than the therapist, if the client is honest in therapy sessions. And, if difficulties arise in the workplace when newly sober, the therapist also offers reassurance and practical suggestions.

From therapy, the sober alcoholic also receives new family communication skills. Years of drinking have often made the alcoholic's family members fearful, resentful, and dissatisfied. With a therapist, the opportunity exists to practice new ways of relating to loved ones.

Improvements in the family's attitude will be observed as their trust in his new-found sobriety increases. However, the therapist will encourage patience in attempting to win these people over. The alcoholic's drinking behavior has probably done much damage to family relationships, and family members will need time to regain their trust.

In the beginning, the stumbling blocks on the alcoholic's road to recovery may be numerous, requiring all the help available. The therapists interviewed for this book unanimously agreed that the most effective treatment for the newly recovering alcoholic is a combination of therapy and active participation in the program of Alcoholics Anonymous.

You may obtain a referral to a therapist who specializes in the treatment of alcoholism and drug addiction from a Chemical Dependency Unit in a hospital near you. For more information and literature regarding alcoholism, you may also contact:

Alcoholics Anonymous World Services, Inc.
Box 459, Grand Central Station
New York, NY 10163

The National Clearinghouse for Alcohol and Drug Information
P.O. Box 2345
Rockville, MD 20852

The National Council on Alcoholism, Inc.
12 W. 21st Street, 7th Floor
New York, NY 10010

Eating and Spending
Help for Two Compulsive Behaviors

*   *Why Twelve-Step programs work* • *What compulsive overeating is* • *Overeaters Anonymous and therapy* • *What compulsive debting is* • *Debtors Anonymous and therapy*

BENEFITS OF TWELVE-STEP PROGRAMS

We all need hope. Many people find hope for a solution to their problems in meetings of Twelve-Step programs, which are based upon Alcoholics Anonymous. These other programs work the same way that A.A. does. People attend meetings, without paying a fee, and listen to the experiences of others who share their problem. They obtain information and literature about the solutions that have worked for other members. They share their difficulties in a receptive and understanding atmosphere, and call other members between meetings for support. And they are encouraged to select a sponsor (someone with experience in recovery) to assist them with the Twelve Steps.

A different group member usually leads the meeting each week, and calls upon other members to briefly share their experience. There are no therapists or doctors present in these meetings, as in group therapy, however.

Here is a look at compulsive overeating and compulsive spending; the popular and successful Twelve-Step programs designed especially for them; and how therapy can be useful in connection with these programs.

EATING DISORDERS

According to Gloria Arenson, the author of *A Substance Called Food*: "Compulsive urges to overeat or gorge and purge may arise as a backlash to strict dieting or fasting, but it is also the inadequate coping mechanism of many people whose lives are filled with stress and loneliness." (P. 19). It is this combination of loneliness and stress that creates the overeater's cycle of repetition, remorse, and despair. And it is through the combination of Overeaters Anonymous and therapy that many people discover the solution that breaks the cycle.

How You Can Tell if You are a Compulsive Overeater

If you answer "Yes" to three of more of the following questions, then you may have a problem with compulsive overeating:

- Have you failed to stay on diets?

- Is your overeating interfering with your job or your home life?

- Do you eat alone to comfort yourself?

- Do you ever feel guilty about the secretive nature of your overeating?

- Do you think about food to the point of obsession?

- Do you overeat when you are angry, disappointed or disillusioned?

- Do you vomit after overeating, on purpose, in order not to gain weight?

- Do you overeat when you are not hungry, because you feel powerless to stop?

If you identify with these questions, and if your medical doctor has given you a clean bill of health, you may be interested in attending meetings of Overeaters Anonymous. Founded in 1960, Overeaters Anonymous is a program of recovery from the emotional aspects of an eating disorder. It is not a diet club or an exercise facility. There are no dues or fees for joining O.A.; the only requirement is the desire to stop eating compulsively, no matter *what* size you wear. O.A. members are treating their overeating problems one day at a time, just as recovering alcoholics abstain from drinking. If there is no listing in your telephone directory for Overeaters Anonymous, feel free to request literature from:

Overeaters Anonymous
P.O. Box 93870
Torrance, CA 90503

Therapy has proven beneficial in the treatment of overeating as well as for other eating disorders such as *anorexia* (dieting to the point of malnutrition and starvation) and *bulimia* (overeating and then dieting, fasting, purging, or vomiting in order to avoid gaining weight). There are several inpatient eating disorder units across the country now which specialize in the appropriate therapy to assist clients with their underlying conflicts, once their eating disorder is controlled. Outpatient therapy, with a professional who is familiar with eating disorders, is also available in many cities throughout the United States. Here is how therapy functioned as a necessary tool in the recoveries of four compulsive overeaters.

Eating to Endure Life

We all need to eat to *sustain* life. But Sandra believed her compulsive overeating was necessary in order to *endure* life. As an adolescent, she began secretive binging to repress her normal fears about scholastic issues, dating, and social activities. As a young adult, Sandra began overeating as a reaction to the perplexities of college life; as a substitute for the boyfriend she felt was missing in her life; as a daily reward after a difficult exam or a good grade; as a way to keep a lid on her anger; and, finally, as an island of oblivion from self-hate and depression.

When Sandra became obese, her parents insisted she enter therapy for the treatment of her overeating. Her therapist suggested that she also begin attending meetings of Overeaters Anonymous.

Once Sandra became abstinent from compulsive over-eating, by following the suggestions she heard at O.A. meetings, she and her therapist were able to explore the underlying issues of loneliness and frustration Sandra felt in college and at home. Her self-esteem increased as her therapist stressed consistency and honesty in her daily behavior and in the reporting of her weekly events to him.

She kept a food journal, for example, and she read it to her therapist every week. This journal consisted of a list of everything she ate, everything she wanted to eat but resisted, and her thoughts and feelings preceding her fantasies about overeating.

This journal enabled Sandra and her therapist to explore the specific situations in her life which were causing her stress. Her writing provided Sandra with insight into her stress reaction patterns and, in time, led her to confront the stress *before* her overeating went out of control.

As she felt her alliance with her therapist build, she became able to express her need for closeness to her parents in a direct and appropriate manner. This openness removed many of Sandra's excuses for secretive eating rituals to repress her old family resentments. With persistence, Sandra successfully used O.A. and therapy to alter her eating patterns and to approach her emotions more directly.

Surrendering Old Beliefs and Illusions

When Julie's husband died of a heart attack, she went to work at a small property management company. Two years later, she quit smoking and she entered menopause, both of which altered her metabolism rate, increased her appetite, and caused her to gain weight. Also, she began overeating compulsively every time she confronted her indecision about whether to leave her job and return to school. Julie attributed her eating disorder to the combination of these three issues.

She entered therapy for help with her eating, which she believed was out of control. But with her therapist, she also began to pursue one small career step at a time. She continued to work part-time as an office manager while she attended real estate school three evenings a week. As the months went by, both Julie and her therapist began to realize that she possessed the stamina to maintain this schedule, but her overeating was still out of control.

Her therapist helped Julie to uncover and discard her father's belief that "women should be seen and not educated." Part of Julie had unconsciously accepted that belief, and when she aspired to more education, she felt conflicted, and turned to food for self-comfort.

Julie also began to date, for the first time since the death of her husband. In therapy, she learned that one of the ways she had kept herself at a distance from men, even though she *told* herself she wanted a relationship, was to insulate herself with her overweight. As she began to lose weight, she expected to feel better about her femininity and her sexuality, and to move easily into the dating world.

What she encountered instead was anxiety and depression. Her therapist then suggested she surrender her illusions about what it meant to be thin. They included:

Illusion: *Thin women have no problems with men; they get everything they want from a man if they'll do what he wants.*

Illusion: *If a man is in charge, promotions and success come more easily to thin women; they don't have to work as hard.*

Julie began to realize that what had kept her from dating men was not her weight, but her mother's internalized warning that "men are only after one thing." She also confronted her fear of intimacy and of a close relationship, as well as some residual guilt and grieving over the loss of her husband. With the help of her therapist, and her participation in Overeaters Anonymous, Julie achieved a comfortable abstinence from compulsive overeating.

"If I Could Have Stayed a Child"

It was alarming to learn, in researching this book, that anorexia is killing thousands of people in this country every year. The terror that you will lose anything that matters, if you turn into the young woman you were meant to become, drives some girls to the edge of death, and some beyond. Gabrielle was spared, but barely.

Gabrielle was thirteen years old when she began to overeat. She was fifteen when she began to starve. Her binging started when she failed to make the gymnastics team at school during the first round of fall tryouts. As she put it:

> *My dad looked so disappointed, when I told him, that I wanted to die. What I did was, I ate three loaves of French bread and butter, and then I remembered that, if I threw up, I wouldn't gain weight. . . . I had heard some older girls talk about it and I really wanted to make that team. If I got fat, I knew I'd fail my dad again and I couldn't stand to see that look on his face. I knew I had to succeed next time. He's been practicing gymnastics with me in our back yard since I was six!*

Gabrielle did succeed in making the gymnastics team the following spring. She was happy, her father was happy, the coach was thrilled with her performances, and for a time, Gabrielle had no problems with overeating. In fact, "It never occurred to me to overeat; my life was perfect."

At age fifteen, Gabrielle developed a healthy, increased appetite and she began to lose her childlike physique. Her coach cut her from the gymnastics team because he felt she was too distracted to concentrate. Her father withdrew his affection from Gabrielle, distancing himself from her. Despite her mother's attempts to comfort her, Gabrielle saw her father's moving away as her punishment for having become a young woman:

> *I needed my dad and he just wasn't there. I felt like if I could have stayed a child, he would have been there.*

When she turned sixteen, Gabrielle stopped eating most of the time. She was failing in several classes. She had isolated from her friends. She was throwing away the food her mother served. She was abusing laxatives to keep from gaining weight. She weighed herself many times a day. Her face had assumed a skull-like appearance. Her ribs were noticeably protruding. She was experiencing heartbeat irregularities. She was obsessed with retaining a childlike physique. And she had fainted from hunger on several occasions.

Following a call to their family physician, Gabrielle entered an eating disorders unit and she began to attend meetings of Overeaters Anonymous in the hospital. Once she was released, Gabrielle continued to attend O.A. meetings, in order to find young women with whom she shared similar issues and felt comfortable. Also, Gabrielle and her parents entered family therapy together, where her father was able to confront his fears:

> *Not knowing how to touch my daughter in a way that wouldn't seem to be sexual, or scare her, as she—you know—became more of a woman. That's why I backed off, I know, not because I don't love my daughter.*

The family therapist was able to introduce Gabrielle's father to new ways of relating to his teenage daughter, and father and daughter were able to share deep feelings for one another in therapy. These skills have carried over into their daily life. Gabrielle was able to let her father know how much she still needed him:

> *But I won't always be able to do stuff, just to get your attention. I feel like I'm not enough for you to be with, if I'm not competing or bringing home awards. That hurts me.*

The family therapist encouraged Gabrielle to begin pursuing activities that interested her, rather than doing what she felt would win her father's approval.

And Gabrielle's mother was able to become more trusting of her daughter:

> I want to search her room for diet pills, and I still worry, but I don't invade her privacy. I hope she'll come to me to talk.

This family has hope, because they are using the preferred form of therapy for their situation—a family setting in which everyone contributing to Gabrielle's difficulties is present and willing to help. Because the entire family is viewed at one time, family therapy is useful in treating each person's contribution to the belief system that has brought the anorectic or bulimic individual to therapy.

When Men Have an Eating Disorder

Women with eating disorders know the cycle of binging, dieting, purging, frustration, resentment, and self-pity. In desperation, they turn to food for comfort, perpetuating the very merry-go-round they have tried, and failed, to break. What is less well-known is that many men suffer from the disease of compulsive overeating and they, too, suffer alone.

Many therapists can tell you of the male client who eats breakfast at home, eats breakfast again during working hours, eats lunch, eats dinner before going home, eats dinner at home, and, before bedtime, sneaks out for more food. Compulsive overeating is not a female disease, but what often prevents men from entering treatment for eating disorders is their feelings of shame.

A Lie He No Longer Needed

Therapy was a vital tool in Sid's recovery from compulsive overeating. The focus of Sid's therapy was his low self-esteem.

I weighed 300 pounds when I finally went to therapy for my overeating problems. I had been in therapy two other times, first to pacify my wife (who left me anyway) and then to get my mother off my back (who kicked me out of her house anyway). But I wasn't willing to give up my overeating, so I don't think therapy could have helped me.

The first place my new therapist sent me was to Overeaters Anonymous. In the suburbs of Chicago, where I live, I thought O.A. was for women. 'Hell,' I said, 'I'm not telling these women I eat four meals at night because I'm lonely.' What happened is, I got so damn lonely, keeping my shame to myself, that I just burst into tears one night in the meeting, and shared my feelings with some of the women there. Then I found other meetings, during the day near work, where there were some men. Now I know I'm not alone with my loneliness or my fear, and I never have to sit home and overeat because of those feelings again.

O.A. provided Sid with a fellowship of people who understood his compulsive overeating. Once he was abstinent, he was able to make good use of therapy to resolve his deep-seated issue of low self-esteem. Every time Sid would criticize himself in therapy, his therapist would disagree with his assessment. His therapist consistently presented Sid to Sid as a valuable, hard-working, deserving human being, no matter what Sid said or did.

At some point, Sid realized that his therapist simply did not see him as an inadequate person. He decided, at that point, that he was either going to have to give up his therapist or give up touting around his inadequacies. He decided to keep the therapist. When he had been in therapy still longer, Sid realized his low self-esteem came from a lifelong inability to assess his worth appropriately. Once accepted by him as a lie he no longer needed, Sid's low self-esteem ceased to be a stumbling block. He successfully terminated his therapy but he still attends O.A. meetings regularly, to help maintain his abstinence from compulsive overeating.

Recovery from their eating disorders was not easy for Sandra, Julie, Gabrielle, or Sid. Each of them remained in therapy for several years, examining their feelings of loneliness and anxiety, and their mistrust of themselves and others. They walked through some discomfort to arrive at a peaceful level of abstinence from compulsive overeating. But eventually, for each of them and for many others, attendance at meetings of Overeaters Anonymous, in conjunction with supportive therapy, provided a solution to the loneliness of their eating disorders.

COMPULSIVE SPENDING

As a culture, we seem to want "more" of everything, and "more" often costs more than we earn. The problem of personal debt is shared by a large portion of our society. Many people are chronically in debt and are regularly up to the limit on their credit cards.

Author Ray Hoskins, in *Rational Madness*, states, "the belief that material items are the major path to happiness and meaning is damaging. . . . The symptoms of addiction are most prevalent in this worship of materialism. There is a challenge ahead to overcome, individually and collectively, this slavery." (P.80). The inner emptiness underlying this materialism and compulsive debting, of which Hoskins speaks so clearly, is addressed effectively in therapy when combined with meetings of Debtors Anonymous.

How to Tell if You're a Compulsive Spender

Here are some indicators of a problem with compulsive spending:

- The act of buying or spending makes you feel better, no matter what item you purchase.

- You buy things you don't need, impulsively, and you don't know why.

- You hide what you buy, and then you lie about it.

- You never seem to have enough of anything to make you feel really good, no matter how much you spend.

- You feel more important, or euphoric, when shopping; spending alters your mood.

- You spend money you really need for something else, and then end up unable to pay your bills.

- You argue with others or lose sleep over your spending habits.

- You are unable to resist the impulse to spend money, just to get rid of it.

- You feel better knowing you have credit cards, even though you are in debt.

If you have struggled with this cycle of denial and discouragement, you may find solutions in Debtors Anonymous.

Debtors Anonymous

Debtors Anonymous is a Twelve-Step program, based on Alcoholics Anonymous, with chapters in Paris, Washington D.C., New York, Chicago, Boston, Miami, San Francisco, and Los Angeles. This program offers meetings where members share their experience with compulsive spending and offer you their phone numbers, for support between meetings, and valuable free literature.

You don't have to be poor or in debt to qualify for, and participate in, Debtors Anonymous. No matter what you earn, if you are chronically in debt, you're welcome there. You're also welcome, and can be helped to change, if you are *never* in debt, and you earn more than enough money to meet your obligations, but you are never able to spend anything on yourself. Members of Debtors Anonymous assure me that such self-esteem issues crop up at nearly every D.A. meeting.

Many people are so caught up in compulsive spending that they lack funds for the necessities of life. Experienced D.A. members will help you bring that problem under control by offering you a plan for meeting your immediate financial needs and repaying money owed.

Included in the solution may be letters to creditors suggesting partial debt repayment plans you can realistically afford. D.A. recommends a "one-day-at-a-time" approach to abstinence from compulsive spending. Members are encouraged to attend meetings regularly; to identify their daily, weekly and monthly spending needs; to write down their expenses and income in a cash journal; to call fellow members for support instead of engaging in compulsive spending; and to use a sponsor for help with the Twelve Steps.

You may obtain more information, or learn how to start your own D.A. group, by writing to:

Debtors Anonymous
General Services Board
P.O. Box 20322
New York, NY 10025-9992

You will know, by attendance at several D.A. meetings, whether your compulsion is to overspend, or to remain unnecessarily in debt, or to deprive yourself unnecessarily. Many compulsive spenders engage in all these behaviors alternately. Whatever your compulsive behavior with money, once it is arrested one-day-at-a-time by attendance at regular meetings of Debtors Anonymous, a therapist can be helpful as you begin to deal with the issues beneath the compulsion. Here are two people's stories about compulsive spending; for both, therapy was an integral part of recovery.

He Was Given Things Instead of Parenting

Like many compulsive spenders, Roger did not come from an impoverished background. He had all the necessities of life and he could recall childhood trips to a summer home, owning a car at 16, and enjoying plenty of spending money. He had always experienced both his parents as emotionally inaccessible to him, however, and he felt he had never really resolved his relationship to either of them.

Roger's behavior with money eventually led to difficulties with numerous bill collectors, one personal bankruptcy, and two condominiums lost to creditors. By the time he sought help in Debtors Anonymous, he was also facing the threat of federal imprisonment for income tax evasion.

Roger entered therapy ostensibly to deal with what he considered to be his fiancee's unreasonableness regarding his compulsive spending. He had no convincing arguments for her regarding his behavior with money, so he sought help to end the dissension between them.

His therapist focused routinely on the reality that no amount of material gain would have eliminated the emotional pain of Roger's incomplete relationship with his parents. Although he resisted this at first, Roger later said he believed it was true, and he elected to remain in therapy not for his fiancee, but in order to change his behavior with money.

It was painful, in therapy, for Roger to confront his childhood feelings of emotional loss regarding both parents, but it was necessary. He understood that he had been given "things" instead of parenting, and that he had continued to use "things" in order to feel loved as an adult.

While Roger processed his feelings of loss from childhood, however, his life marched on, and it required attention. Roger used his therapist as a weekly check-in center to discuss his spending habits; what he was learning in his D.A. meetings; the progress of his relationship to his fiancee; and how he felt about his new behavior with money.

Roger's therapist noted that Roger displaced his old feelings of rage onto present-time situations such as his impending marriage, because doing so made him feel less vulnerable than grieving his childhood losses. But because his therapist was vigilant, and because Roger continued to attend D.A. meetings, he has completed that old grieving, and he has not had to substitute another addiction for his former compulsive spending, which is often a problem for people with addictive personalities.

Jane's Spending Was a Cry for Help

Like Roger, Jane had reached the maximum limit on her credit cards and had borrowed heavily from friends and from loan companies, under assumed names, without revealing her behavior to her husband, Frank. She was bright and well-educated but, when she married Frank, she resented leaving her job as an advertising copywriter to maintain their home and raise two children.

At first, she justified her excessive shopping as being a necessary duty she owed to Frank—the image of the upwardly mobile Boston social couple. By the time she sought help in therapy she was spending the household food budget, the insurance money, and their emergency fund, all on clothing and jewelry for herself. When her anxiety surrounding her secretive behavior became great enough, Jane sought the help of a therapist "before Frank caught me!"

The first thing Jane revealed to her therapist was the depth of her feelings of inadequacy, no matter how full her closet was, or what she was wearing on any given day. In therapy, she was also able to express, rather quickly, her ambivalence at having left a promising career to raise the family she dearly loved. And she was keenly aware of her anger for her husband because he had not noticed her "cry for help" behavior.

Two years into therapy, with regular attendance at meetings of Debtors Anonymous, Jane returned to copy writing part-time, and learned money management skills to assist her in running her household appropriately. She likes her job and she is enjoying being a homemaker as well as a writer again. It took longer, but she and Frank were also able to develop direct communication skills which have improved their relationship. Frank's trust in Jane had been eroded but it has been repaired, slowly, as she has demonstrated new reliability with money.

Her therapist made several suggestions to Jane which were particularly valuable for her situation. He indicated that she appeared to feel depressed whenever she went shopping and could not buy anything, so he suggested she shop only once a week; that she take someone with her, in the beginning, for support; that she make a conscious commitment to limit herself to the items on her shopping list; and that the list always include something that Jane really wanted for herself, and that cost less than $25.00, to lessen her feelings of deprivation.

Today, Jane's self-esteem is not determined by her clothing and jewelry. It comes, instead, from the personal integrity she derives from her behavior with money and her return to creative work as a writer. And because of her increased self-esteem, she no longer feels the urge to spend money excessively in response to her old feelings of inadequacy.

If you have an eating disorder, or you engage in compulsive behavior with money, the combination of a Twelve-Step program and therapy is a highly successful treatment solution.

Section Four

The final chapters of this book deal with loss and with saying goodbye. Included is a look at the stages of grief, and how your therapist will help you with grieving. What happens in grief workshops is also described. You will learn what to do if your therapist dies when you are in treatment, and why it is important to deal with your own mortality in therapy. A writing exercise will be suggested to help you gain closure to a relationship that has ended. Finally, you will learn how to approach the process of termination from therapy and what that process is like.

CHAPTER
10
Letting Go

• The stages of grieving, what to expect from a loss, and how therapy helps • Grief workshops • Why losing a parent to whom you were not close is painful • Letters to help complete losses • What to do if your therapist dies.

HEALING YOUR LOSSES

Grief is what we go through to heal from the pain of a loss. It applies not only to the feelings connected to a death, but also to those feelings that accompany the disappointments of daily living. When you lose someone or something important to you, your entire life is affected.

Many people don't want to feel loss because it is painful. But you must, because it won't go away. Often, grief that is unacknowledged turns into depression if you ignore it. Some physical complaints are also caused by an unwillingness to release one of life's treasures. Physicians know that, when you "hold on," your body tenses up and functions less effectively. You *can't* walk away from grief. It becomes a wedge between you and your loved ones. It can interfere with your effectiveness on the job. And it can even edge out your healthy reasons for living.

When you think of grief, you may think first of the losses of people close to you. But losing a job or retiring; moving to another neighborhood, school, or city; or letting go of a long-held belief are also losses.

People undergoing medical surgery are told to anticipate pain and to accept the fact that they won't regain their full physical strength for some time. However, people rarely allow themselves to recover from a severe emotional loss in a soothing, recuperative manner.

The three people mentioned below complained of depression when they participated in my consumer workshop on selecting and using a therapist. What they shared in common was unprocessed grief.

When Dottie's mother died, Dottie was unable to cry; she had stoically gone about the business of settling her mother's estate. Since the funeral, she had been awaking with a numbing depression. Her daughter successfully encouraged Dottie to participate in a grief workshop. There, she began the process of actually accepting that her mother was gone.

When Jack's wife, Nelda, developed Alzheimer's Disease, at age 72, Jack became severely depressed. Although he had accepted her presently, deteriorating condition in a realistic manner, his therapist also enabled

him to experience and grieve his yearnings for his ener-
getic and joyful young wife. His depression improved
when, in therapy, he was able, additionally, to accept his
own advancing years, about which he had much denial.

Melinda received a promotion with a design firm in her
hometown, which required a move from Ohio to Los
Angeles. In L.A., she loved her work and she loved her
new apartment; she made friends easily; and she was satisfied with the relocation. But three months after her move,
she developed a mild depression. Early in therapy, she attributed this temporary sadness to missing her former
home, neighbors, friends, and business associates. Therapy
clarified her feelings. Time, and long-distance phone calls,
eased the longing.

In addition to the above-mentioned losses, the following
experiences will often trigger feelings of depression, until
you identify and process the loss. Did a close friendship
recently end? Are you dieting and do you miss your non-
diet junk food? Have you recently quit smoking? Are you
newly widowed, separated, or divorced? Are you hanging
on to an old idea about life that no longer works? Can you
think of any significant losses for which you never really
grieved at the time of the loss?

Bereavement opens up many sensitive issues. If you
choose to enter therapy specifically for the purposes of
help with grief, look for the traits of empathy and compassion in a grief counselor. You will know, in your early sessions, if this counselor is a nonjudgmental individual who
can support your grieving process. This person should be
soft-spoken, gentle, and kind to you. Other important
qualities are sensitivity to the issues grief has opened up

within you, and the ability to help you to recognize them. This counselor should be able to assist you in the integration of your loss as you move on with your life.

The following stages of grief don't always occur in sequence but, in one way or another, you are likely to touch on each of them in the grieving process.

Denial

Denial is the "anesthesia" of the human emotional system. At first, you may feel so numb that you act as if the loss had not occurred.

Emotional Upheaval

You may experience powerful emotions as you become aware of your painful loss. At some point, you'll probably feel angry at the unfairness of your loss, or at who or what you've lost, for deserting you. You may also feel some anxiety as the loss produces changes in your own life, or feelings of abandonment.

Grief and Your Body

Don't be surprised if minor physical illness follows a loss experience. Your body may respond to the loss by temporarily malfunctioning.

Guilt

Feeling guilty is often preferable to having no explanation at all for the unthinkable occurrence of your loss. It helps to remember that your loss doesn't have to be anyone's *fault*.

Reentry

Loyalty to a memory, or to some fixed idea about how long grief "should" last, may temporarily delay your return to normal activities. It is usually helpful to use your own inner sense of what is appropriate, in reentering work and social activities. This is your loss, and no one else can really hold you to a "schedule" for grieving.

Laughter

When someone you love is no longer with you, part of what you remember is bound to be funny, as you recall the idiosyncracies that made that person loveable. Just like your tears, laughter is one of your body's releases for pent-up tension and grief.

Hope

Hope has a way of slipping through the cracks and taking root again, in spite of your feelings of grief. You resume your life and you find, surprisingly, that you have survived the loss.

The Imprint of Your Loss

If it was a major loss you may not get over it completely. Grieving alters the mourner and it leads to new, inner strength. It gives you a deeper capacity for feeling compassion for others. And, being human, it's impossible to believe any of that at the time of your loss. Sometimes, you will just have to trust that others you know have survived a loss, until that strength comes to you, too.

GRIEF WORKSHOPS

After a significant personal loss, a grief workshop may be suggested to you by your therapist. These workshops are led by a counselor specially trained to assist you in the grief process.

A grief workshop is an emotionally safe setting, much like your therapist's office. That feeling of security is important because many people are afraid, after the loss of a parent, spouse, or child, that, if they start to mourn, the dam will burst and there will be no stopping their grief.

If you are a man, you may find it particularly awkward to reveal these deeper feelings. But when grief overtakes you in spite of your attempts to contain it, just allow yourself to heal without shame or embarrassment. Life's losses don't exclude men as recipients, and everyone has a right to grieve.

In grief workshops, you are encouraged to talk about the lost person and what he or she meant to you. You will be given techniques to help you separate from the dead individual, such as bringing a photo of that person to the workshop to formalize your goodbye. Gradually and gently, you are helped to accept that your experience with the lost person has ended. You will find the words, with the help of a skilled counselor, to say goodbye to the loved one you have lost.

The process of grieving takes time. The purpose of a grief workshop is to enable you to *begin* it. But with some losses, such as the untimely loss of one's child, there is a lifelong wound that never goes away. The child's birthday or special family days may evoke periodic grieving so long as the parent is alive. Al and Barbara lost their only daughter, Linda, at age fourteen in a drowning accident in Washington state. As Al tells it:

I felt as if a truck was crushing my chest all day, every day, for many months. I learned in my grief workshop that I <u>had</u> been crushed. I was crushed that I couldn't bring Linda back, and by the grief I kept inside. Nothing this bad had ever happened. I never really felt I said goodbye to Linda because we were advised not to view her body, since it had been in the water three days.

When the sheriff's deputy came to our door with Linda's watch that I gave her for junior high graduation, my wife came completely apart. I comforted Barbara, but I couldn't cry. For that reason, my time in grief counseling was long, a couple of years. I just couldn't get to my feelings, but I kept going to the group. I work on the ship loading docks in Bremerton, and I sure didn't want to break down in front of those guys.

One night, into my grief workshop comes this girl, Lucy, about Linda's age. She lost both parents in a small plane crash in New Mexico, and she can't cry. She just can't ever cry. She sat there with her head down every week and fidgeted with her hands. Everyone else tried to draw her out, but I hated her there. She made me nervous. I resented Lucy, because she was alive and Linda was dead.

My therapist told me to stay in the group, so I did, but I felt like a chump. One night, I watched the kid staring at her hands like always, and I just went across the room and put my arms around her. No words, nothing. I don't even know why. But it wouldn't stay down anymore, it all poured out. I will miss my daughter every day of my life, but now that I think about it, that's when some healing began.

COMPLETING THE PAST

There is another kind of loss for which therapy is extremely valuable: the curiously painful feelings that occur when you lose a parent to whom you were *not* close. Rick and his father had a distant relationship when Rick was growing up. Rick felt he had never really been connected to his dad.

When Rick's father passed away, Rick attended his father's funeral out of respect for his mother. He was shocked at the depth of his reaction to his father's death:

There was so much grief inside of me I feel absurd and inauthentic even telling you about it. After all, shouldn't I really be celebrating? I'm better off without that lousy son-of-a-bitch. Aren't I? I know I am! He was never any use to me! Right?

Rick learned in therapy that he *did* feel a genuine sense of loss, not so much for the absence of his father, but for the loss of hope. As Rick put it:

It was over, and it was over in a big way and it never really happened at all because we never did get close, and yes, I was cheated. And yes, I had to grieve.

With the loss of a parent to whom you were never close, there is as much grief as there is in adults who lose a beloved parent. If you had a physically abusive parent, or a cold and distant parent, in therapy you will be encouraged to grieve the lost hope about that relationship, just as Rick did.

THINGS UNSAID

When you lose someone you love, and you feel anything was left unsaid by you, your pain is accompanied by regret, and sometimes by guilt. Although it is not the same as facing the person, there is a feeling of closure to be gained by writing that person a letter. It can also be helpful to share this writing with your therapist. Your writing reveals clues as to how much grieving you have yet to do, and it allows you the benefit of sharing your pain with one who has gotten to know you well.

Richard was 19 years old, and working in Australia, when his older brother passed away. Here is the letter he wrote when he received the news of his brother's death:

Dear James,

I cannot believe that I can't pick up the phone and hear your voice on the other end. I know you didn't want me to take this job, but I'm as bullheaded as you are, or were. There are so many things I didn't say to you. Like how you taught me to be responsible even when I didn't feel like it, and how you taught me to shoot baskets even when you didn't feel like it. Your unmerciful teasing when I got a terrible haircut. I shared the same bedroom with you, I looked up to you, there was nobody like you, and I don't think I'll ever get used to this. You were the best brother anyone could have. I hope I remembered to say it. But in case I didn't, here it is.

A death is the end of a life, but it is not the end of a relationship. Richard was able to share his letter with his pastor and, in brief pastoral counseling, he received much comfort and understanding about the impermanence of life. If, like Richard, you lose someone close to you, you will always carry some memories of the loved one within you. If the final parting requires some formalized ritual, write that person a letter. Anything unsaid, even "I cared," need not remain so. With a therapist, you have an ideal opportunity to write and share whatever is in your heart and on your mind, for the closure you require.

THE LOSS OF YOUR THERAPIST

If your therapist passes away while you are in treatment, it will be essential that you grieve, and also that you remain on your own journey into emotional maturity. Patricia related her experience, following the death of her therapist:

Dr. Woods, my therapist, was almost like a really good mother. I was on an important journey with her, learning to live a full, successful life. We had repaired a lot of old damage and I felt good about what we had accomplished.

*And although we had not discussed it, I think I was prob-
ably about ready to terminate. The day before my appointment, I got a telephone call informing me that my therapist had died. Her daughter told me that I would be welcome at the memorial service.*

*How could Dr. Woods be dead? Maybe it was a mis-
take. Maybe it was another Dr. Woods. Maybe it was true.
I couldn't take it in. I went to the service, but I didn't
know anyone and I felt worse. I got so depressed I had to
find another therapist. The only thing I wish we had talked
about, I mean Dr. Woods and I, was I wish we had talked
about death. Mine and hers. We never did. With my new
therapist, it's the <u>first</u> thing I talked about.*

*I'm glad I went back into therapy. Actually, I feel pretty
good these days. But I can tell you, I'll never forget that
phone call. I think the client and the therapist both hope
therapists aren't going to die. But they do. I'm here to tell
you they do.*

If your therapist dies, leaves practice, retires, or moves
away, it is often helpful to continue the process on which
you embarked by finding another therapist, as Patricia did.
Most therapists will leave a referral to another available
therapist, and it may help you to pursue such a referral.

Whatever you do, it will comfort you to continue your
own growth in the face of your loss. You probably covered
a lot of ground with that therapist. You may be tempted
to believe that, because your therapist is gone, your work
has also vanished. Those doubts are just a natural, temporary reaction to this loss in your life. But what you

learned in therapy, you will always own. It is yours to use, and this loss cannot invalidate it.

11

Saying Goodbye

- *Acknowledging your own mortality* • *Firing a therapist*
- *Termination from therapy.*

LIVING NOW!

You have only one real choice about life, and all the other therapy work you do leads up to it. You can walk through life just passing time or you can leave some expressions of your enthusiasm for life, and some evidence that you worked and lived and loved here. But, no matter what your age now, the illusion that you will *never* run out of time will rob you of the opportunity to live as fully as possible. That's an expensive illusion. How and why you come to discuss your mortality with your therapist is up to you, but its inclusion in your treatment, at some point, is essential.

Therapy can be an ideal arena in which to review your life, accept the past, repair its damage if you can, and move into the action *today*. Your present life is where you will end up, in therapy, no matter where you started. It's where you really live, one day at a time, and it's where the freedom and the fun are located. Really feeling alive is dependent, to some extent, on your acceptance that you won't always be alive.

IF YOU FIRE YOUR THERAPIST

For most people, therapy works effectively with few problems between therapist and client. Occasionally, however, two people just aren't a match. Let's say you don't feel your therapist is helping you to reach your goals, after a year; or is someone who really doesn't have positive feelings for you. Your therapist is, after all, an individual with a personality and a way of relating that is different from yours.

If your expectations aren't being met in therapy, and you aren't looking forward to your sessions most of the time, maybe it's appropriate to look for another therapist. No therapist is right for everyone. So if, after a year, you are still trying to adjust to your therapist instead of getting any other work done, you have nothing to lose by leaving, and you might hit it off with someone else right away.

But beware of yourself if you don't get along with, say, three or four therapists in a row. Then you have several interesting options. You can make (and keep!) a commitment to remain with the therapist you are currently seeing, for a specific period of time agreed upon by the two of you. Another option is to see whether you manage better on your own than in therapy. Either you will decide you *can* manage without a therapist, or you will go back, stick it out, and commit to making the changes you want to make.

If neither one of those options is appealing, just stay in therapy and do it! Your indecision about whether to stick with a therapist, or to go it alone, may be keeping you from the *real* business at hand, such as looking at something in your life that badly needs attention.

TERMINATING THERAPY

Termination from therapy comes when you and your therapist mutually agree that it is time for you to move on. You will arrive at this decision after a thorough discussion. What you have formed, together, is an important partnership. You won't want to bolt out the door in a huff, or inform your therapist by mail, telegram, or telephone that you won't be back. If, during your therapy, you have the urge for such a premature departure, you will want to discuss these feelings with your therapist, who can help you to understand why. But, for the purpose of termination, you sit together, like always, and talk about what the work and the relationship have meant to both of you.

Terminating your therapy is also important because it is a rehearsal for learning to say goodbye to other people in your life. What you learn from a healthy parting with your therapist equips you to separate from others in your life when it is appropriate, and in a considerate, mature manner.

The questions below are derived from my interviews with clients who have successfully terminated their therapy by mutual agreement with their therapist. For each of these clients, the termination discussions varied considerably, and you will certainly add other issues to the list when termination arises for you.

1. Why do I think I may be ready for termination at this particular time in my therapy?

2. In discussing termination at this time, do I have any self-destructive motives, such as avoiding certain issues?

3. If so, what are they?

4. What did I find especially valuable about my work here?

5. Is there anything I now think the course of treatment should have focused on more emphatically?

6. Do I feel satisfied that I have gotten everything for which I came to therapy?

7. How has knowing my therapist, as a person, affected my life and changed me?

8. Is there anything my therapist feels I should remain to work on?

9. Do I think I would want to be in group therapy, or some other form of treatment, now? Why?

10. How does my therapist feel about my being in another kind of therapy?

11. Am I willing to leave the door open, in case I need to return to my therapist?

12. Is my therapist willing to leave that door open?

13. Are there any problems I came to therapy to resolve, and have discovered are just part of the human condition?

14. What are these issues?

It is important that you agree upon a termination date with your therapist and then stick to it. This date makes the termination a reality for you both. He can more effectively plan your final sessions, and the date imposes a certain amount of healthy pressure on you to complete your current therapy business.

Many professionals advise against "open-ended" termination because they say it causes anxiety and an unsettled feeling within clients. Clients don't know whether to go or stay, how much longer to stay, or how to decide that. For these reasons, a blurred termination can be confusing, even though you may find that you suddenly very much want to stay. If you liked going there, it's understandable you might want to linger. But when your mission has been accomplished, it's best to say goodbye, with a little sadness and a great deal of gratitude. In most instances, your are encouraged to remember that you can check in again, at any time.

Termination is a time when you both reflect upon your therapy and the effective, responsible adult you have become as a result. Talking about your progress in termination reinforces it and you move on fairly comfortably. A send-off from someone who really knows you, who has helped you, and who likes you, is a well-deserved morale booster.

Termination is somewhat like leaving home. It is leaving old damage and wounded feelings behind you, and getting to take all the wisdom and other good stuff with you. For all these reasons, termination from therapy is worth doing thoroughly.

Whenever and however you leave, you will probably think about and miss your therapist once in a while. Once in a while, your therapist will do the same: wondering how you are, what you did about a particular situation when it came up in your life, be glad your therapy was helpful. And, yes, miss you. Because the bond never goes one way, it goes both ways. That's why it works.

Afterword

I believe that dedicated therapists and willing patients who work together to change *one* human life also alter the world and contribute to peace. I am deeply grateful to all the clients and professionals who helped me write this book.

If you're breathing, there's hope, and a compassionate place for you to work things out at your own pace. Growing pains are necessary, but much suffering and loneliness is optional. Wherever you are, you really do matter, and someone is willing to help you. Why not give yourself a gift and let your personal journey into solutions begin today?

References

Ackerman, Robert J. and Pickering, Susan E., *Abused No More*, Blue Ridge Summit, PA: HSI/TAB Books, 1989.

Alcoholics Anonymous, New York: Alcoholics Anonymous World Services, 1976.

Arenson, Gloria, *A Substance Called Food*, Blue Ridge Summit, PA: HSI/Tab Books, 1989.

Hoskins, Ray, *Rational Madness*, Blue Ridge Summit, PA: HSI/TAB Books, 1989.

Pollard, John K. III, *Self Parenting: the Complete Guide to Your Inner Conversations*, Malibu, CA: author, 1987.

Index